Soundings
A journal of politics and culture

Issue 53
Where next?

Editors
Sally Davison & Ben Little

Editorial Board
Stuart Hall
Joe Littler
Doreen Massey
Michael Rustin
George Shire

Reviews Editor
Jon Wilson

Art Editor
Tim Davison

Editorial Office
Lawrence & Wishart, 99a Wallis Road, London E9 5LN

Advertisements
Write for information to Soundings, c/o Lawrence & Wishart

Subscriptions
2013 subscription rates are (for three issues):
Institutions £140, Individuals £35

Collection as a whole © Soundings 2013
Individual articles © the authors 2013

No article may be reproduced or transmitted by any means, electronic or mechanical, including photocopying, recording or any information storage and retrieval system, without the permission in writing of the publisher, editor or author

ISSN 1362 6620
ISBN 9781907103872
Cover Photo © Bjorn Steinz Panos

Printed in Great Britain by Halstan, Amersham
Soundings is published three times a year, in autumn, spring and summer by:
Lawrence & Wishart, 99a Wallis Road, London E9 5LN.
Email: info@lwbooks.co.uk

www.soundings.org.uk

Contents

- 4 — Editorial
- 8 — After neoliberalism: analysing the present
  Stuart Hall, Doreen Massey and Michael Rustin
- 23 — The state of the left
  Andrew Gamble
- 33 — Green shoots? Interview with Natalie Bennett
  Jo Littler and Susanna Rustin
- 44 — Why it's still kicking off everywhere
  Paul Mason
- 56 — Railways - beyond privatisation
  Paul Salveson
- 69 — Leveson and the prospects for media reform
  Deborah Grayson and Des Freedman
- 82 — Revisiting the Olympic legacy
  James Graham, Bob Gilbert, Anna Minton, Mark Perryman, Gavin Poynter and Claire Westall
- 93 — In France, will change be now or never?
  Gavin Bowd
- 103 — A connected society
  Danielle Allen
- 114 — Reviews
  Neal Lawson, Ken Spours, Ed Wallis and Mike Waite
- 129 — Has multiculturalism in Britain retreated?
  Varun Uberoi and Tariq Modood
- 143 — When is peace?
  Cynthia Cockburn

Editorial

Neoliberalism and how to end its dominance has been a central concern in *Soundings* since its inception. In this issue, we carry the framing statement for our online manifesto, *After neoliberalism?*, written by the journal's three founding editors, Stuart Hall, Doreen Massey and Mike Rustin.[1] The aim of the manifesto is to focus attention on the nature of the neoliberal settlement, including the social, cultural and political battles that have attended its emergence and maintenance - and those that might help bring about its demise. It argues that mainstream political debate largely avoids confronting the systemic failures that underpin the financial crash, preferring to believe that normal service will shortly be resumed. And as long as this belief continues, political debate will centre on the extent to which state spending should be cut rather than on how to secure a political economy in which all of us have enough to live on, and a society in which the common good displaces profit as the ultimate goal.

As Andrew Gamble notes, Labour saw its vote drop below 30 per cent in 2010, amid a widespread sense that it had been responsible for the economic regime that had brought about disaster, and that it had few ideas for future change. His prescription for a renewed Labour Party has three main elements: a focus on extending democracy and constitutional reform; a rethinking of its ideas about cultural and national identity; and a drive to associate the party with creativity in the economy, especially through green technology. Andrew acknowledges that this is a difficult task but judges that Ed Miliband is taking steps in the right direction. In this vein, the Labour Party Policy Review process can be understood as a welcome attempt to think through the necessary conditions for creating a new economic and political settlement for Labour and the country. We are cautiously optimistic that this will help shift current debate on to more promising terrain for the left.

Natalie Bennett, the new leader of the Green Party, believes that her party occupies the large political space that was vacated when New Labour shifted to the right. And she argues that Labour continues to be too cautious on many issues. For example on education it has not come out against free schools, and its academies policy in many ways opened up the way for current Tory practice. And although

Editorial

it could be argued that the Green Party has the luxury of not needing to look like a government in waiting, it is also true that a lingering attachment to a privileging of choice over equality, and to competitiveness as a key way to achieve success, is evidence of the entrenched difficulty of moving away from the New Labour legacy. Natalie herself is not hopeful of real change in Labour, and suggests that the Greens are the way forward for those who seek a sustainable future and social justice.

Paul Mason has no doubts about the depth of the current crisis, and thinks that we are witnessing a global revolt against neoliberalism, especially from young people who believe that the system has failed to secure their future. This has been aided by the communications revolution, which assists the development of horizontal and networked groups. He believes that most critics of this kind of organisation are shaped by a time when there were 'structured, hierarchical movements with a clear counter-narrative and demands'. This time has now passed, and current movements reflect the new realities as well as the nature of contemporary working life - fragmented, short-lived, ephemeral, lacking ties. But in spite of this the social movements are seeking to develop a counterpower within capitalism, and ways of living differently. And given that neoliberalism is indeed incapable of delivering a secure future, it is likely that things will continue to kick off.

We believe that dialogue between such different positions is crucial. It is important - not to say self-evident - that critical politics takes many different forms. There are no easy answers to the task of challenging the dominant consensus, and direct action and campaigns within civil society will play a role in this, as will a diverse analysis and actions by some of the smaller parties. This is by no means to diminish the crucial contribution needed from the Labour Party, without whom there is no realistic prospect for change (or at least not in England).

The next two articles engage with specific issues through analysis that connects political action and winnable change with a wider challenge to current common sense. Paul Salveson argues that John Major's 1993 railway privatisation was driven purely by ideology; the railways at that time were by and large well-run and efficient, while privatisation has seen a rise both in subsidies from the tax-payer and costs to the traveller, as well as failures of safety and maintenance while money is siphoned off rather than invested. Paul then shows how a centre left strategy for the railways could change all this - through a new strategic body, making the constituent parts of the current system more accountable, and the gradual taking back of control

Soundings

of franchises as they come up for renewal. This would be combined with a renewed emphasis on community railways and an attempt to wrest control of rolling stock away from the banks, who currently own the lion's share of this most profitable part of the privatised system. In short, Paul shows how an incoming Labour government could transform the railways gradually, without significant costs, and with increased community involvement and popular support, at the same time as making an argument about why profit seeking is detrimental the running of the system.

Deborah Grayson and Des Freedman discuss another area where the left has an excellent and popular case to make - in favour of public scrutiny in the face of powerful media corporations. They argue that the government's response to the Leveson Report - brought into being through campaigning by Hacked Off and *The Guardian*, as well as the political courage shown by the Labour leadership in speaking up for the popular view - will show whether or not the corporations have been able to win simply through the exercise of their lobbying power. They also place ownership at the centre of the debate: democracy needs wider media ownership as well as legal protections (both to protect people against the press and to defend press freedom). Here is another winnable cause that challenges the dominant view.

Elsewhere in the issue, our roundtable discussion on the Olympics explores how deeply the Games were enmeshed in rhetorics of competiveness, spectacle and private-sector led regeneration. Gavin Bowd ponders whether the new French government will have the courage and strategy necessary to carry out its programme in the face of neoliberal European obstacles. Danielle Allen demonstrates the importance of connectedness to political equality (yet another reason to deplore the apartheid tendencies of Tory cuts to housing benefits). Varun Uberoi and Tariq Modood argue that it is misunderstandings of the meaning of multiculturalism that have been largely responsible for the view that it is in retreat, and that in fact most contemporary leading politicians have made statements in support of inclusivity. Finally Cynthia Cockburn documents the steadfastness and endurance of women in organisations in Northern Ireland, Bosnia-Herzegovina and Israel-Palestine, who battle for peace in the face of overwhelming odds.

This issue has been edited by Sally Davison and Ben Little, the new *Soundings* co-editors. We plan to keep on developing the journal in the critical and pluralist spirit

Editorial

it has established over the last eighteen years, and wish to express here our great appreciation for the tremendous contribution to the project that was made by our predecessor and colleague Jonathan Rutherford.

Note

1. The 'manifesto' will be developed over the next year in monthly instalments, freely available online at www.lwbooks.co.uk/journals/soundings/manifesto.html. Extended versions of some pieces will be reproduced in the journal.

After neoliberalism: analysing the present

Stuart Hall, Doreen Massey and Michael Rustin

The founding editors of Soundings set out the framing analysis for our online manifesto.

———

With the banking crisis and the credit crunch of 2007-8, and their economic repercussions around the globe, the system of neoliberalism, or global free-market capitalism, that has come to dominate the world in the three decades since 1980, has imploded. As the scale of toxic debt became evident, credit and inter-bank lending dried up, spending slowed, output declined and unemployment rose. The system's vastly inflated financial sectors, which speculate in assets largely unrelated to the real economy of goods and services, precipitated an economic crisis whose catastrophic consequences are still unfolding.

We believe that mainstream political debate simply does not recognise the depth of this crisis, nor the consequent need for radical rethinking. The economic model that has underpinned the social and political settlement of the last three decades is unravelling, but the broader political and social consensus apparently remains in place. We therefore offer this analysis as a contribution to the debate, in the hope that it will help people on the left think more about how we can shift the parameters of the debate, from one concerning small palliative and restorative measures, to one which opens the way for moving towards a new political era and new understandings of what constitutes the good society.[1]

For three decades, the neoliberal system has been generating vast profits

After neoliberalism: analysing the present

for multi-nationals, investment institutions and venture capitalists, and huge accumulations of wealth for the new global super-rich, while grossly increasing the gap between rich and poor and deepening inequalities of income, health and life chances within and between countries, on a scale not seen since before the second world war. In North America and Western Europe - hitherto dynamos of the global economic system - rates of growth are now lower than during the early post-war decades, when there was a more even balance of power between the social classes. There has been a steep decline in manufacturing and a hot-house expansion of financial services and the service economy; and a massive shift of power and resources from public to private, from state to market. 'The market' has become the model of social relations, exchange value the only value. Western governments have shown themselves weak and indecisive in responding to the environmental crisis, climate change and the threat to sustainable life on the planet, and have refused to address the issues in other than their own - market - terms.

Likewise, the financial crisis has been used by many Western governments as a means of further entrenching the neoliberal model. They have adopted swingeing 'austerity measures' which, they claim, is the only way of reducing the deficits generated during the bonanza period of the 1980s and 1990s. They have launched an assault on the incomes, living standards and conditions of life of the less well-off members of society. In the UK, the cuts programme has frozen incomes, capped benefits, savaged public sector employment and undermined local government. It has encouraged private capital to hollow-out the welfare state and dismantle the structures of health, welfare and education services. The burden of 'solving' the crisis has been disproportionately off-loaded on to working people, targeting vulnerable, marginalised groups. These include low-income, single-parent families; children in poverty; women juggling part-time employment with multiple domestic responsibilities; pensioners, the disabled and the mentally ill; welfare-benefits and low-cost public housing 'dependants'; the young unemployed (especially black youth); and students. Youth facilities have been closed; and citizens who depend on public amenities for their social well-being find themselves bereft. Apart from its punitive and regressive social effects, this is a strategy destined to fail even in its own terms, since its main consequence will be a serious fall in demand and a collapse of tax revenues, deepening the downward economic spiral, with little fall in the deficit.

In other words, the crisis itself has been used to reinforce the redistribution from poor to rich. Moreover, it has also provided the alibi for a far-reaching further restructuring of state and society along market lines, with a raft of ideologically-driven 'reforms' designed to advance privatisation and marketisation. It has encouraged private, individualised solutions to social problems. This makes it all the more important for the left to make the argument that it is time for a new moral and economic settlement.

Global dimensions of neoliberalism

This neoliberal hegemony, both in its pomp and in its crisis, has had global implications. Dynamic, expanding capitalist systems have their own strategic and geopolitical imperatives. Neoliberalism has sought a favourable climate towards business across the globe. It demands low tax regimes, limited state interference, and unimpeded access to markets and vital resources. It calls for internal security, the capacity to contain external enemies, and strong rulers in control of their populations, with whom bargains can be struck and influence exercised. It engenders hostility to more democratic and alternative experiments. These principles have guided the strategies and underpinned the network of alliances, blocs and bases that the West - led by the US - has constructed. The Middle East clearly demonstrates that maintaining generally favourable conditions of operation - securing spheres of influence (the US/Israel alliance), dealing with military challenges (Iran, Pakistan), repressing political instability (the Horn of Africa) and defeating threats (the Taliban, al-Quaida, Afghanistan) - figures as much as do specific resource 'grabs', such as for oil (Iraq, the Gulf States).

The particular global character of neoliberalism was part of its initiating armoury - for instance through the Washington Consensus from the 1980s onwards - and it is also an element of its historical specificity. It is a globalisation in which a new form of financial imperialism is crucial (and London has been central in its invention and dissemination), and in which a key dynamic has been a planetary search for new assets in which to speculate (through, for example, exported programmes of privatisation, spiralling markets in commodity futures, the buying up of vast tracts of land).

But neoliberalism never conquered everything. It operated within, and created, a world of great diversity and unevenness. Its early - classic - laboratory was Chile,

After neoliberalism: analysing the present

but the rise of South East Asian tigers was, critically, a state-aided development (by no means the official neoliberal recipe). And in spite of the Western triumphalism of 1989, Russia also retains its specificities - a hybrid of oligarchic and state capitalism combined with authoritarianism. China, too, struggles to define a different model; it currently combines centralised party control with openness to foreign investment, and acute internal geographical dislocations and widespread social conflict with break-neck rates of growth and the lifting of hundreds of millions out of poverty. Indeed, conflict has erupted in many parts of the world where the neoliberal orthodoxy has been adopted. India, so frequently lauded for its embrace of the market consensus, exhibits both extraordinary rifts between the new elites and the impoverished, and multiple and persistent conflicts over its current economic strategy. Other major sites of conflict have been the water and gas wars in Bolivia, and the struggle of 'the poors' in Thailand. The emerging articulations of progressive governments and grassroots social movements in Latin America are, in varying ways and in varying degrees, responses to the impact of previous neoliberal policies. The alter-globalisation movement has been vocal. This has not been a simple victory.

In fact, its very diversity and conflict has been an element in neoliberalism's current fracturing. The economic (im)balance between China and the USA has been both a central mechanism of complementarity and, increasingly, a source of instability. The crisis in the Eurozone has also been a critical weak link in the global structure. Having failed to design a financial architecture that could address uneven development between constituent countries, the Euro-elite powers (the troika above all) now attempt to blame the inevitable disaster on the constituent countries themselves (or some of them). They thus set peoples against peoples, provoking dangerous nationalisms, while the culpability of the elite is effectively obscured. It is a geographical conjuring trick that converts the political frontier from being one between conflicting economic and social interests into one between national peoples, and moulds those peoples' self-identifications along nationalist lines.

Meanwhile, and over the longer term, a tectonic shift of economic power is taking place, to China and the other BRIC countries, bringing with it growing confidence and increasing claims for voice on the world stage. Trade, and indeed conversations and contacts more generally, increasingly bypasses the North Atlantic region altogether. At the same time, while the number of millionaires increases even in the poorest places, in many countries, most obviously in sub-Saharan

Soundings

Africa, there is rising impoverishment, widespread malnutrition (partly a product of the speculation in food prices), ecological devastation and political instability. There are battles over the control of energy and mineral resources. In the face of overwhelmingly unfavourable external pressures and restraints, governments cannot deal with poor schooling, hunger, malnutrition, disease and health pandemics or resist western consumerism, the arms traders and freelance mercenaries.

The 'squeeze' has triggered an increase in local, tribal, inter-ethnic and religious sectarian violence, civil wars, military coups, armed militias, child soldiers, 'ethnic cleansing' and genocidal rape; and these in turn have precipitated cross-border and international migration, as civilians flee war-zones, join refugee camps or seek asylum abroad. The 'failed (or failing) states' which Western strategists proclaim to be a major threat to security are themselves often the perverse consequences of neoliberalism and western intervention. And the very concept of failed state is often used as an ideological weapon.

Most recently, the response to the crisis by the North Atlantic elites has made matters worse - for instance through its effects on prices and currency levels. The fact of global instability and looming crisis has by no means modified the neoliberal offensive. If Chile was the laboratory for the early phases, Greece has become the laboratory for an even more fierce implementation, while the Arab Spring may yet be recuperated to open up new fields for market forces. And in Latin America the recent US-sanctioned coups in Honduras and Paraguay have been swiftly followed by radical concessions to foreign capital.

Ideologies and conflicts

The present economic crisis is a moment of potential rupture. The welfare-state 'settlement' that preceded the neoliberal era in the North Atlantic world had crumbled in the 1970s, and, with the end of the Cold War, Thatcherite and Reaganite neoliberalism won the contest over which way forward would be taken. This outcome was not inevitable. Conflicts between social settlements and the crafting of hegemonies are the product of contending social forces. During the welfare state era, the working class did make economic gains. Wealth was modestly redistributed, egalitarianism and social rights became more embedded. Capital's share of the surplus was significantly eroded. But this was a shift that could not be

After neoliberalism: analysing the present

tolerated. The expanded globalisation of its operation was partly (among its many determinants, and along with privatisation and financialisation) a means of restoring the declining share of the surplus taken by capital. Resistance to Thatcherism's 'war on society', conflicts over democratic government in London and other cities, struggles in the global South, the rise of new social movements, opposition to the poll tax, and contests over the rights of organised labour everywhere - all these were critical moments in the struggle to determine what would follow. Social forces locked in conflict across different areas of social life have always been at stake.

The current neoliberal settlement has also entailed the re-working of the common-sense assumptions of the earlier, social democratic settlement. Every social settlement, in order to establish itself, is crucially founded on embedding as common sense a whole bundle of beliefs - ideas beyond question, assumptions so deep that the very fact that they *are* assumptions is only rarely brought to light. In the case of neoliberalism this bundle of ideas revolves around the supposed naturalness of 'the market', the primacy of the competitive individual, the superiority of the private over the public. It is as a result of the hegemony of this bundle of ideas - their being the ruling common sense - that the settlement as a whole is commonly called 'neoliberal'. But while commitment to neoliberal economic theory is a key part of the overall consensus, it is also the case that the theory itself plays a crucial role in legitimising the restoration and reinvigoration of a regime of power, profit and privilege.

As we have seen, the rubrics of neoliberalism, embedded in a common sense that has enrolled whole populations materially and imaginatively into a financialised and marketised view of the world, are implemented when they serve those interests and are blithely ignored when they do not (the bail-out of the banks being only the most recent and egregious example). Likewise its attacks on the state and on notions of the public are propelled not just out of a belief in an economic theory but from the hope that they will lead to the reopening of areas for potential profit-making through commodification. This drive to expand the sphere of accumulation has been crucial to the restoration of the old powers.

Origins and explanations

Neoliberalism has its origins in eighteenth-century liberal political theory and political economy, from where it derives its touchstones. It has been revamped and reworked to be appropriate to these times and geographies, and it is multiple in form in reflection of these expanded geographies. But its core propositions, of the free possessive individual engaging with others through market transactions, remain the touchstone. From the very beginning these propositions were the product of class interests - in the UK in the eighteenth century, of the rising agrarian, commercial, and later manufacturing, bourgeoisies. The attempt has always been to present them as eternal truths - concepts of markets and individuals being merely descriptive of an ideal state of nature. That this was not so has been demonstrated over centuries, as the 'free market' and the free-standing individual have had to be actively produced and imposed. Whether through Acts of Enclosure, impositions of 'structural adjustment', military interventions or attacks on public expenditure, market societies are products of intervention (and often by states).

That market forces are imposed on some but not others has been true since the colonial metropole's 'free-labour' regimes were harnessed by the imperial system to the 'forced-labour' of plantation slavery. This contradiction became more evident when they collided in the slave revolts and the struggles over Abolition. Market forces are never universally imposed. There is no such thing as a fully marketised system. Capitalism relies on monopolies and 'socialised' risk, and on spheres that exist outside the logic of its operations - including that of the reproduction of people, and the natural world. Free wage-labour has always been augmented by unfree forms of exploitation such as serfdom, slavery, bondage, indenture, peonage. These mark the limits of 'the market's' generalisability.

Indeed, much of what has gone on through globalisation over the last thirty years resonates with events in late eighteenth-century and early nineteenth-century England, when industrial and urbanised capitalism was first finding its form. The expulsion from their land of millions in the global South recalls the enclosures of the commons. The vast migrations to the ever-expanding cities are like the migrations of earlier industrialisations (these within-nation migrations being just as socially disruptive and potentially explosive as migrations between nations). There is the creation of a vast new force of 'free labourers' with all the personal and social wrenchings (as well as new freedoms) that that can entail, and the further commodification of land and labour. International migration itself (in part a result of all of these developments and their attendant geographically uneven ramifications) represents the creation of a free global labour force - just as the age of the Swing

After neoliberalism: analysing the present

rioters and of Peterloo saw the creation of a national labour market in Britain.

Meanwhile, looking as it were in the opposite direction, from the UK outwards, while successive governments hang pathetically on to the coat-tails of a USA whose economic hegemony is itself under challenge from China and the other BRIC countries, the City of London - again building on its long assumption of supremacy, but now thoroughly internationalised and one of the fountainheads of neoliberalism - has found itself, at least for a while, a new imperial role.

Neoliberalism's project, then, is a reassertion of capital's historic imperative to profit - through financialisation, globalisation and yet further commodification.

Causes and complexities

It is never easy to define what is cause and what is effect in conjunctures of this kind. There are legitimate differences of view about the causal emphasis that should be allotted to ideological, political and material factors, or the weight that should be given to the conscious actions of social classes versus the dynamic attributes of social structures. The picture is never simple. It is certainly true that class interests have been active in imposing neoliberalism on the world, and now refuse to concede the relative gains of the past three decades; and it is also the case that classes have shared economic interests - both those that are particular to specific sectors (for example, agriculture or manufacture), and those that are general - concerning the maintenance of stability and a favourable climate in which to 'do business'.

However, the shift in economic and social power over the decades since the 1970s was not driven by a single motor. The economic is critical; but it cannot determine everything - even 'in the last instance', as Althusser famously argued. Any given conjuncture represents, rather, the fusion 'into a ruptural unity' of an ensemble of economic, social, political and ideological factors where 'dissimilar currents ... heterogeneous class interests ... contrary political and social strivings' fuse.[2] What has come together in the current neoliberal conjuncture includes class and other social interests, new institutional arrangements, the exercise of excessive influence by private corporations over democratic processes, political developments such as the recruitment of New Labour to the neoliberal consensus, the effects of legitimising ideologies and a quasi-religious belief in the 'hidden hand', and the self-propelling virtues of 'the market'.

Soundings

Classes are also formations with complex internal compositions that change over historical time. Those among whom neoliberalism became the dominant tendency now constitute a global class that includes - alongside older echelons - the world's leading industrialists and businesspeople, CEOs of the great corporate firms, the new transnational, trans-ethnic speculators, directors of large financial institutions, hedge-fund operators, venture capitalists, as well as the senior executives who manage the system and have a major stake in its success. We must add, too, the key but subaltern archipelago of consultants, marketing experts, public relations people, lawyers, creative accountants and tax-avoidance experts whose fortunes are tied to its success. No doubt the huge privileges and immunities won by this formation explain why they seem so morally denuded, impervious to any sense of a wider community or responsibility for their actions, and completely lacking in any understanding of how ordinary people live. Their resistance to reform has been obdurate, their greed brazen. They reward themselves extravagantly, while insisting that 'we are all in this together', and that their real purpose is 'serving customers' and 'corporate responsibility', not protecting their own interests.

Of course, the term class interests does not imply that classes are monolithic, that they appear on the political stage as unified actors, or are fully conscious of their interests and pursue them rationally. There are important conflicts of interest (for instance in the UK between, say, those of finance capital and those of small businesses, northern manufacturing and small farmers). These real contradictions may offer political opportunities. Furthermore, interests are always open to conflicting ideological interpretations, and their redefinition can have political effects.

Nor is economic class the only salient social division. Gender, racial, ethnic and sexual divisions long predate the birth of capitalism, and still structure social relations in distinctive ways. They have their own binary categories (male/female, masculine/feminine, straight/gay, religious/secular, colonial/metropolitan, civilised/barbarian), and they figure differently from class in the distribution of social and symbolic goods (though they are articulated to class). They 'manage' their own systems of reward and scarcity (paid/unpaid, legitimacy/illegitimacy, normal/abnormal, saved/damned). They position the bodies of their subjects differently in the Nature/Culture continuum. They 'govern' different moments of the life-cycle

After neoliberalism: analysing the present

and attribute to people different subjective capacities (paternal/maternal, emotional/cognitive, duty/pleasure).

These social divisions each have privileged sites of operation (for example, home/workplace, private/public) and distinct disciplinary regimes (patriarchal power, property inheritance, unpaid domestic labour, control of sexuality, gendered and racially-differentiated wage rates). They deploy different modes of oppression (religious persecution, social and sexual discrimination, racialisation). They construct their own hierarchies of 'othering' and belonging, via discrimination, stereotyping, prejudicial speech, inferiorisation, marginalisation, abjection, projection, fantasying and fetishisation. When these social divisions operate within a capitalist system, they are, of course, profoundly shaped by it and articulated to it. But they retain their 'relative autonomy'. This requires us to rethink social relations from another perspective (for instance reframing the exploitation of labour in production from the perspective of the reproduction of social labour, which is heavily gendered). These divisions have been reworked through the present settlement, sometimes being reinforced and sometimes refashioned in ambiguous ways.

Thus, a general social and political heterogeneity is evident in the protest movements against the austerity cuts. They have been spearheaded in Britain by professional organisations as well as by the unions. New social movements like UK Uncut, Feminist Fightback or Occupy are characterised by complex class, gender and ethnic composition. The Green Party provides a bridge between environmental movements and mainstream politics. Mobilising resistance thus requires alliances of a sort which only a multi-focused political strategy can hope to construct.

Common sense, identity, and culture

Ideology plays a key role in disseminating, legitimising and re-invigorating a regime of power, profit and privilege. Neoliberal ideas seem to have sedimented into the western imaginary and become embedded in popular 'common sense'. They set the parameters - provide the 'taken-for-granteds' - of public discussion, media debate and popular calculation.

Not all of this, though, is specific to the neoliberal settlement of recent decades. Even during the redistributivist welfare state, the basic tenets of free-market capitalism were not fundamentally challenged. Redistribution transformed the lives of millions, but its project remained ameliorative. The very language of politics revealed this: we 'intervened' (i.e. took conscious social action) into 'markets' (i.e. the naturally pregiven state of affairs).

One key strand in neoliberalism's ideological armoury is neoliberal economic theory itself. So 'naturalised' have its nostrums become that policies can claim to be implemented with popular consent, though they are manifestly partial and limited. Opening public areas for potential profit-making is accepted because it appears to be 'just economic common sense'. The ethos of the 'free market' is taken to licence an increasing disregard for moral standards, and even for the law itself. Commercialisation has cultivated an ethos of corruption and evasiveness. Banks, once beacons of probity, rig interest rates, mis-sell products, launder drug money, flout international embargoes, hide away fortunes in safe havens. They settle their 'misdemeanours' for huge sums that hardly dent their balance sheets. Similarly, when private firms that have been publicly contracted fail to meet targets they are allowed to continue. Graduates stacking supermarket shelves are told they don't need to be paid because they are 'getting work experience'. Commercialisation permeates everywhere, trumps everything. Once the imperatives of a 'market culture' become entrenched, anything goes. Such is the power of the hegemonic common sense.

But it is a common sense that has to be produced and maintained. The capture of political influence by corporate wealth and power serves to maintain their hold over the political process and state institutions (as in the phone-hacking/*News International* scandals). Corporate ownership of dominant sectors of the media gives capital sway over the means and strategies of representation: the retinue of CEOs, public relations people and lobbyists who haunt the TV studios to reassure us that 'things have been put in place to prevent it happening again', have guaranteed access, and function as the primary definers of reality. Contrary views have a more fleeting visibility. A few intrepid journalists do an impressive job of unmasking, but the media more generally seems to find itself thinking within the groove of the prevailing neoliberal orthodoxies. Even where 'balance' is provided, this rarely questions the prevailing terms of debate, and there is usually a reluctance to pursue with any rigour the serious issues involved.

The ideology of competitive individualism has also been imposed via the stigmatisation of the so-called 'undeserving' poor. 'Welfare scroungers', who cannot

After neoliberalism: analysing the present

provide for themselves through their own efforts, are labelled morally deficient - 'idlers who prefer a lie-in to work', 'living on benefits as a "life-style" choice'. Similarly, everyone - parents, students, clients, patients, taxpayers, citizens - is expected to think of themselves as consumers of 'products' that will bring them individual economic advantage, rather than as social beings satisfying a human need, producing something of use, or participating in an experience of learning from which others as well as themselves may benefit. In these ways, neoliberalism has been engaged in constructing new entrepreneurial identities and re-engineering the bourgeois subject.

Looking at the broader cultural picture, we detect similar tendencies: in consumer and celebrity cultures, the drive for instant gratification, the fantasies of success, the fetishisation of technology, the triumph of 'life-style' over substance, the endless refashioning of the 'self', the commercialisation of 'identity' and the utopias of self-sufficiency. These 'soft' forms of power are as effective in changing social attitudes as are 'hard' forms of power such as legislation to restrict strikes.

It is the reassertion of the powers of capital that has produced the neoliberal world as we know it today, as its agents have taken command of the new circuits of global capital. The widening of inequalities is the main launch-pad of this restoration bid. And this has put into question the long-promised transfer of income, power and responsibility from rich to poor, men to women, centre to margin. Countervailing values - equality, democracy and citizenship - have been circumvented, and dissenting social forces fragmented and dispersed. The reinvigorated finance sector has been articulated with a new imperialism. These 'victories' are flaunted in brash material form - each new high-rise a middle finger raised.

The future of the crisis

This phase of free-market capitalism has now entered a serious economic crisis from which it cannot easily engineer an exit. But the shape of the crisis remains 'economic'. There are so far no major political fractures, no unsettlings of ideological hegemony, no ruptures in popular discourse. The disastrous effects of the crisis are clearly evident; but there is little understanding of how everyday troubles connect to wider structures. There is no serious crisis of ideas. Indeed the crisis has been exploited as a further opportunity to reinforce the very

Soundings

neoliberal narrative that has led to the system's implosion, and to push its project even further. Neoliberals dogmatically insist that it was the 'restraints' on, not the excesses of, the market that bear the responsibility for its manifest failure. Extensive work, backed by daunting resources, has gone into securing consent to this version of events. There are forensically targeted attacks on groups like Occupy London, the very unpretentiousness of whose tents, huddled between the monumental edifices of Mammon and God, gave it symbolic power. Its questions resonated. It had to go.

And yet, there is no hegemonic closure - hegemonies, even the neoliberal one, are never totally secure. Materially, the cuts bite deep and hard, and there are more to come. There is growing distress, discontent, de-politicisation, scepticism and loss of confidence in the political class. The distress is palpable. But people feel puzzled about where to go next. Polls suggest that the drive for privatisation has not won the day: but are egalitarianism and social collectivism still alive and well? There is a sense that something is wrong with a system which distributes wealth in a 1% - 99% way. Politicians feel obliged to reassure the public daily that the cuts are 'fair'. There are other such resonances in popular consciousness. But who is nurturing them?

Farther afield, in Europe, there is popular dissent, opposition to austerity strategies and support for 'growth-and-jobs' alternatives. There is the democratic awakening of the 'Arab Spring' and, in Latin America, explicit challenges to neoliberal hegemony. Hegemonies are never completed projects: they are always in contention. There are always cracks and contradictions - and therefore opportunities.

However, in the UK, Labour, the official opposition, is in serious difficulties. It leads in the polls but it is not yet winning hearts and minds. It shuttles between conflicting ways forward. It seems afraid of its own (left) shadow, in hock to the old Blairite rump and a belief in the conservatism of the electorate, trapped in parliamentary rituals, mesmerised by electoral politics. It has been rendered speechless by the charge that it opened the door through which the Coalition is triumphantly marching. It seems unable to draw a clear line in the sand: a political frontier. It makes effective tactical interventions but appears tongue-tied when invited to enunciate an alternative set of principles, to outline a strategic political approach or to sketch out a compelling alternative vision.

After neoliberalism: analysing the present

A 'manifesto' by instalments

Our purpose is to set out an agenda of ideas for a progressive political project which transcends the limitations of conventional thinking as to what it is 'reasonable' to propose or do. We will try to open a debate which goes beyond matters of electoral feasibility, or of what 'the markets' will tolerate. Electoral change *is* urgent, critical and necessary: but it will not change much if it means a continuation of the existing assumptions under a different name. As to practicality - 'what works affects lives' - yes, but there must be a fundamental break with the pragmatic calculations which disfigure current political thinking. It is the maps, not the facts, which have disintegrated. The neoliberal order itself needs to be called into question, and radical alternatives to its foundational assumptions put forward for discussion. Our analysis suggests that this is a moment for changing the terms of debate, reformulating positions, taking the longer view, making a leap.

For us, this is not a question of restoring the tried remedies of the post-war welfare-state settlement. Of course, that would not be an altogether bad place to start. But that compromise, for all its attempt to achieve a different balance of values and power from that dictated by markets, nevertheless accepted that the market sectors should still be left essentially free to generate profits, while a public system managed by elected governments would merely be allowed to redistribute some of the ensuing resources, and provide for some social needs which markets would otherwise neglect. (And by the 1970s, as the left itself argued, some of the other flaws of the welfare settlement, for example the state's frequent paternalism and lack of responsiveness, were contributing to the ebbing away of support.) The rise and crisis of neoliberalism should have taught us that that historical solution was not radical enough. In any case the political conditions of existence of the previous social democratic settlement are no longer operative. Debating how and why the terms of reference have changed is certainly worth doing. But such debate will only be fruitful if new transitional demands, framed in the light of the analysis of contemporary global realities, point us further ahead.

This is a slightly edited version of our After Neoliberalism: the Kilburn Manifesto. *The 'manifesto' will be developed in monthly instalments, freely available online at www. lwbooks.co.uk/journals/soundings/manifesto.html. We hope to engage in this project not*

Soundings

only friends and colleagues who have been closely associated with Soundings, *but also a much broader public. We invite comments and reflections on this whole idea and its formulation. For more information (including on why Kilburn!), please go to the website.*

Notes

1. Regular *Soundings* readers will recognise that this is a case we have been developing for some time. For more background to these arguments see our online book *The neoliberal crisis*: www.lwbooks.co.uk/ebooks/The_Neoliberal_crisis.pdf.

2. Louis Althusser, *For Marx*, Verso 1969, Part 3, 'Contradiction and Overdetermination', p99.

The state of the left

Andrew Gamble

Labour's priorities after Blair and Brown

Labour lost office in 2010 after thirteen years in government - the longest stretch of Labour government the party has managed since it was founded a hundred years ago. It more than doubled the previous record, and was marked by three general election victories, the first two, in 1997 and 2001, by decisive margins, at least as measured by parliamentary seats. At long last it appeared that Tony Blair and Gordon Brown had succeeded where Clement Attlee and Harold Wilson had failed, transforming Labour from a party of opposition into a party of government. One sign of this was that although the party lost in 2010 it did not suffer the kind of splits that had taken place after its defeats in 1951, 1970 and 1979. The party has remained remarkably united. The leadership election in 2010 did not offer stark choices between the main candidates, and, with some wobbles, the party united behind its new leader, who has gradually increased in confidence and effectiveness. The party no longer appears to be ideologically divided in the way that it was for most of its twentieth-century history.

The election defeat in 2010 was, however, serious. Labour saw its vote share fall below 30 per cent, for only the second time since 1945, and much of the ground captured by New Labour, particularly in the South of England, was ceded. The loss of seats was less marked, however, and the Conservatives narrowly failed to secure an overall majority. After a shaky post-election start Labour's fortunes began to improve, helped considerably by the lack of in-fighting: a party that can stay united after it has been defeated in a general election is in a strong position to renew its leadership and its policies, and to be a credible alternative at the next election. And the opinion polls during 2012 moved firmly in Labour's direction, giving the party steady if not overwhelming leads over the Conservatives. The Liberal Democrat vote crashed in the first year of the Coalition government, and by 2012 had still

Soundings

not recovered. But the Conservative vote held up remarkably well until the end of 2011, with Cameron's standing running far ahead of that of the Labour leader. However this all changed in 2012. The government suffered major losses in the local government elections, and the Conservatives now saw their support and their reputation for competence nose-dive. This was partly a result of the continuing recession; partly a result of a series of unforced errors, many of them connected to George Osborne's 2012 budget - one of the least politically astute budgets of recent times - and partly a result of Labour emerging as a more effective and credible opposition. By the summer of 2012, two years into the parliament, Labour appeared to be on course for an early return to government.

Yet despite the signs that support is returning to Labour, the mood in the party remains cautious and low-key. There seems to be little excitement around Labour, little positive enthusiasm outside Labour's ranks for an early return of the party to government, and little sense that the party is generating new ideas or approaches. This is leading some commentators to suggest that if Labour wins it will be by default, because of the growing unpopularity of the government rather than because it has found a new winning formula or a leadership that inspires positive support. The negative ratings of all three party leaders and the still modest poll leads of Labour do not suggest an irresistible surge of support towards Labour, and an outright Labour victory at the next election will be hard to achieve. Despite the travails of the government, the Conservatives still have time to rally their forces and win an outright majority at the next election.

All this has led to speculation that the left is facing a crisis of purpose and leadership, and has given rise to concern that even if Labour were to find itself back in government after the next election it would not have a clear programme for government. The tide of opinion and the popular mood still seem to favour the right, amidst the biggest economic impasse since the 1930s. Two possible reasons for this are, firstly, that the left is still traumatised by New Labour, and has not yet found a way to deal with that experience; and secondly, and in part as a consequence, that Labour and the left more generally have so far failed to come up with many persuasive ideas for dealing with the recession. There is a paradox at the heart of left politics. One of the driving forces in the creation and imagining of the left was opposition to capitalism, and in particular the concentration of power and class inequalities with which it was associated. Yet the left has most often prospered when

The state of the left

capitalism has been successful, providing the resources which left governments could then redistribute for social purposes. When capitalism has been unsuccessful the left has often been placed on the defensive, and it is parties of the right, sometimes the extreme and populist right, that have gathered strength.

New Labour's ascendancy was won during the long upturn in the economy between 1992 and 2008. Part of the difficulty for the British left in coming to terms with New Labour today is the scale of New Labour's success in its heyday. New Labour is conventionally dated from Tony Blair's accession to the Labour leadership in 1994, but much of the groundwork had been done under the leaderships of Neil Kinnock and John Smith. Labour's modernising project began in the 1980s after the major electoral defeat in 1983. New Labour represented the climax of the modernising project, but much of it had already been anticipated. This means that a quarter of the party's entire history has been dominated by this particular strand of social democracy, which was characterised by a move away both from democratic socialism and from Labourism, which had been twin pillars of the old party. It is hard for the party to reject the new identity and purpose which New Labour established, yet that is what many in the party yearn to do, so uncomfortable have they become with the legacy from this period.

The wish to repudiate New Labour comes about for three main reasons.

In the first place there was strong disappointment that New Labour did not do more with the opportunities which it had. Its landslide majority in 1997 gave Labour for a time a remarkable ascendancy in British politics. Only after 1945 had Labour seemed to be in a stronger position. But from the outset the government acted cautiously, as though it could not believe its good fortune, believing that it was in a much weaker position than it really was. The acceptance of the outgoing Conservative government's spending plans for the first two years of the new government was one sign of this; others included the timidity over many aspects of constitutional reform, and over joining the single currency. There was also disappointment that the government took so few steps to reverse some of the measures enacted by the Conservatives in the previous eighteen years, being content for the most part to govern within the constraints and parameters established by them. New Labour, it was said, was more interested in accommodating to existing preferences than in shaping them, and playing safe rather than trying to create a different kind of politics and a different kind of society. Some of this disappointment can be put down to expectations which were too high and unrealistic, but it is also a reflection of the lack of ambition and confidence which New Labour exuded. Many of the senior figures in the party had come to believe that the country really was Conservative in its deepest instincts, and that the right-wing tabloids reflected those instincts. To govern effectively Labour had to be aware all the time that it was inhabiting a space where it was not meant to be, and act accordingly. Tony Blair exemplified this attitude more than anyone. A measure of his genius and also of his limitations as a social democratic leader was his skill at representing the median voter. When asked to place political leaders on an ideological spectrum, voters consistently placed Conservative leaders to the right of themselves and Labour leaders including Gordon Brown to their left. But Tony Blair tended to be placed where most voters put themselves.

If the first reason for disillusion was some of the policy choices that the Labour government did not make, the second reason was some of the policy choices it did. Two areas of particular unhappiness were foreign policy decisions, most notably the decision to join the Americans in invading Iraq, and decisions which curtailed civil liberties. Many longstanding members of the Labour Party left because of these issues, particularly the first. On liberal intervention abroad to protect human rights New Labour showed that it had some very firm convictions. This was one area where focus groups and public opinion polls did not hold sway. The strong commitment to supporting the invasion of Iraq greatly damaged Tony Blair's standing both within his party and ultimately within the country. His premiership never recovered, once it became plain that no weapons of mass destruction would ever be discovered, and that Britain and the United States were bogged down in a protracted struggle to maintain security and build a new state, increasingly perceived by many Iraqis as armies of occupation. Blair's strong commitment to the United States after 9/11 and his sympathy with the aims of the War on Terror was fully in line with the Atlanticism which had governed the policies of successive British governments since 1945. But it made him deeply unpopular with a section of his party. If the outcomes of the invasion had been as many expected, then Blair might have had a major foreign policy success, but, as it was, the failure to secure the peace in Iraq after the invasion lost Blair and New Labour much support. This was compounded by the increasingly authoritarian turn the government took towards civil liberties in the aftermath of 9/11. The bombing in London on 7 July 2005 strengthened those in the security state who wanted the police to be given

The state of the left

much greater powers to interrogate suspects without being forced either to charge them or release them. A cross-party campaign developed to oppose New Labour's increasingly tough line on policing Britain and keeping the population safe.

The third reason for the widespread disillusion with New Labour was the shipwreck of its economic policy and its reputation for economic competence at the end of its third term. This had been hard won, and was one of the most obvious attributes of New Labour's ascendancy. Labour repeatedly boasted after 1997 that it had ended the cycle of boom and bust, and delivered an economy which was safe in its hands, and which guaranteed rising living standards through increased wages and increased public spending. To those critics who accused the government of following Thatcherite economic policies and not challenging them, New Labour argued quite plausibly that it was the first government to make combining economic efficiency and social justice a reality. The proof of this could be seen in the introduction of the minimum wage, SureStart, tax credits, the child trust fund and major uplifts in spending on health and education, all undertaken while maintaining an economy which grew uninterruptedly for fifteen years. This was a more powerful story and a more solid record of achievement than many of the critics were prepared to allow. The Conservatives in particular were perplexed because it had been an iron law of British politics that Labour governments always spent too much and quickly precipitated a financial crisis. In the case of New Labour the financial crisis was delayed for ten years.

When the financial crash occurred in 2008 the Labour government under Gordon Brown reacted fairly swiftly and decisively. It helped stave off a major collapse, demonstrating that the state was still able to act as the guarantor of last resort, and remained a crucial stabiliser of the capitalist economy in an emergency. New Labour was initially given some credit for this, but the much bigger story soon became the way in which the crisis had exposed the policies pursued since 1997 as woefully inadequate. The new regulatory bodies which Labour had established had failed to spot the danger of systemic risk in the financial system, and had failed to avert the crisis. Labour in retrospect appeared to have been far too accommodating to City interests, far too ready to praise the City and to encourage light-touch regulation. As the recession deepened, so Labour was increasingly blamed for allowing the situation to develop in the first place. The government lost its lead over the Conservatives for economic competence, which the Conservatives gleefully exploited by arguing that New Labour was just like Old Labour, incapable of being trusted with the government of the economy. Labour was the party which had not mended the roof when the sun was shining, and had spent too much, borrowed too much, and created the biggest structural deficit in the country's history.

Much of this narrative was tendentious and misleading, but it was effective politics, and Labour had little effective rejoinder to it. In seeking to defend an orthodox response to the crisis the Brown government drew attention to its earlier failings. Why had the government not acted sooner to rein in the banks? The Brown government was also unwilling to experiment with radical alternative policies, which might have been its one chance of success. It might have said to the electorate: 'The financial crash has created a new situation. It has invalidated many of the assumptions on which our previous policy was based. We intend to set out a programme of recovery which breaks explicitly with the policies which have been shown to have failed.' Such an approach would have required an acceptance of the need to tackle the deficit, but as part of a policy to ensure growth and a restructuring of many institutions in the British economy - from the financial practices of the City of London to corporate governance and executive pay - and with priority being given to the science base and long-term investment in innovation and skills. Labour made some moves in this direction, but not nearly enough, and the government was handicapped by Brown's very low approval ratings, and also by his stubborn refusal to acknowledge that any cuts in spending were required to deal with the deficit.

Rethinking Labour's strategy

Labour's predicament, and the wider predicament of the left, is to find a way to acknowledge the achievements as well as the failures of the New Labour period, but also then to recognise the very different political circumstances which have come about since the financial crash, which make possible a bolder and more radical vision than New Labour ever embraced. Labour needs a new strategy for government as well as a new strategy for winning power and conducting politics.

Three areas requiring a radical rethink are the constitution, cultural politics and the economy. The constitution is often said to be of no interest to voters, but Labour has frequently ignored the constitution in the past and put itself at a disadvantage. New Labour was unusual in putting through a large number of constitutional

The state of the left

reforms, including significant devolution to Scotland and Wales, partial reform of the House of Lords, freedom of information measures, and restoration of devolved government in Northern Ireland. But Labour's constitutional reforms were incomplete; they were introduced piecemeal, and without any overall coherent plan, so that they created as many anomalies as they removed. Labour now needs some bold and imaginative thinking about the constitution, which will require the sacrifice of some Labour interests. The present relationship between the four nations is unsatisfactory because it is a quasi-federal arrangement in which the advantages of the unitary state have been lost, without the benefits of a full federal union. The decision to devolve powers to Scotland and Wales looks politically irreversible, so movement towards a full federal union looks unavoidable if the United Kingdom is to be held together. Shaping the rules of this new union should be a prime task for the left.

Other areas of unfinished constitutional reform include the House of Lords and boundary changes. Labour has taken up defensive positions on both these questions, refusing to support the timetable motion which could have delivered Lords reform in this Parliament, and at the same time also supporting the Liberal Democrats in attempting to block the proposed reduction in the number of constituencies and MPs, which would help to reduce the current anti-Conservative bias in the vote. A better policy would be to co-operate in enacting a lasting reform of the Second Chamber, and accepting the democratic principle that votes should be equal, while pushing for measures to encourage wider participation. Taking principled rather than partisan positions on the constitution would signal the way in which Labour wants to conduct politics, and would bring great long-term benefits. The extension and deepening of democracy should be a prime task of the left, whether or not it confers immediate political benefits. Labour has put itself in a position where it is supporting both an unelected second chamber and the continuation of electoral bias. Far better to support both reforms, and press for other associated changes, such as rules guaranteeing the preservation of independent members in the House of Lords and measures to ensure higher voter registration and participation.

A second area is cultural politics. The left used to have a very powerful and effective cultural politics, built around the organisations, institutions and communities of the working class. It had its limitations, particularly in relationship to race and gender, but it also generated a deep solidarity. As this has waned, the left has often found it difficult to adapt to new forms of cultural politics, particularly in the field of the relationship between Englishness and Britishness, the dilemmas of multiculturalism, and the emergence of transnational identities, for example with the European Union. An effective electoral strategy must think through issues of identity and belonging, to find new sources of solidarity which can bind the party together. Engaging in these spaces is essential for a successful progressive politics, but they are also generally the most difficult, and as a result are often ignored.

New Labour made some progress on all these issues, and appeared for a time to be building a new and diverse coalition, which attracted voters from many different groups. But the momentum was lost, the coalition began to fragment, and Labour found it increasingly difficult to cope with the issues of Europe, immigrants, Scottish nationalism, Englishness and multiculturalism. It became increasingly defensive, resorting to the kind of negative positions favoured by the tabloids - though it never sounded as if it really believed in them. Its disinclination to provide a positive defence of the European Union, or of immigration, or of the Union has been marked, and this has imposed severe limits on its politics and its appeal.

A third area is the economy. Parties and political leaders are increasingly judged on how they handle the economy, and they come under great pressure to achieve positive results within the confines of the electoral cycle. This tends to make policy-makers extremely cautious, and keen to promote business as usual whenever possible. Radical initiatives in policy are hard to introduce because of the accumulation of entrenched interests which oppose them. The current impasse in the UK economy and in the international economy do, however, create opportunities for radical thinking and for practical experiments, since the established framework of policy is visible failing.

New Labour was not wrong in thinking that a successful economic policy had to combine social justice and economic efficiency, but both terms need reconfiguring. The growth in inequality, the widening gap between richest and poorest, and the stagnation and even decline of middle and low incomes while top incomes have soared has become one of the most marked features of contemporary capitalism. At the same time the possibilities of future economic growth are clouded, both in the short term, by the overhang of debt created by the boom of the last twenty-five years which has brought about the longest recession since the 1930s, and in the long term, by fears of climate change and other environmental dangers that threaten the

The state of the left

sustainability of the industrial civilisation created in the last two hundred years.

For a hundred years the left has been primarily associated with state-led solutions to the problems of market capitalism; and interventions supported by the left over a long period have helped stabilise capitalism politically and ensure its continued growth. The most lasting legacy of these interventions has been the size and scope of the state itself: it continues to expand, creating new entitlements and sectors dependent on it. Much of modern politics is fought over issues to do with the size of the state and the way it establishes entitlements and redistributes resources. The left has become particularly identified with parts of the public sector and public sector programmes, such as health and welfare, while the right is more identified with the military and security. The problem all parties face is that the growth of entitlements exceeds the growth of the fiscal base and the willingness of citizens to pay higher taxes. This crisis of the tax state is not new, but it has acquired a new meaning in present circumstances. Adjusting the fiscal constitutions of modern democracies has become extremely difficult, because the bursting of the financial bubble that sustained the boom implies long years of austerity and increasing hardship for many citizens.

Higher taxes on the rich may increase the sense of solidarity and willingness to make sacrifices, but on their own they cannot deal with the problems of adequate funding of the entitlements which citizens have grown to demand. Parties of the left must either win the argument for much higher taxes on everyone (the Scandinavian model), or they must increase government revenue through the adoption of a new economic model which can generate sustainable growth. Given the long-term environmental dangers the world faces, such a model has at the very least not to make the problems of the environment significantly worse. The interest in programmes such as the Green New Deal is one manifestation of this. The aim is to identify policies capable of generating long-term investment in technologies and infrastructure which can facilitate the adaptation of human societies to the need to preserve the environment, while spreading the benefits of industrial societies to all peoples.

One implication of this approach is that the left needs to be associated with production, with wealth creation, with science and technology. It cannot afford to be portrayed as the party which is only concerned with the distribution of wealth after it has been created. It has to be involved with how that wealth is created. One fruitful line of advance for the left would be to renew its interest in the ecology of enterprises and organisations. It needs to re-engage with the reform of corporate governance, using the powers of the state to create frameworks which will counter monopoly and promote pluralism and diversity in business enterprises.

The left cannot afford to be simply defensive when it comes to capitalism. It needs to recognise that positive action can reshape capitalism and transform it in directions which promote the values and goals of the left, helping to achieve societies which are both more equal and more sustainable. The creativity and energy associated with capitalism are not forces to be resisted but forces to be channelled. In the midst of the worst economic downturn to grip capitalism since the 1930s, the worst outcomes have been averted so far by the way states have responded, and by their determination not to repeat the mistakes of that earlier era. But the international political economy is still deadlocked, and bold measures will be needed by national governments to create the conditions for long-term recovery. This is a great opportunity for the left, but there needs to be some hard thinking and some political imagination if it is to be grasped.

Andrew Gamble is Professor of Politics at the University of Cambridge and author of *The Spectre at the Feast: capitalist crisis and the politics of recession*

Green shoots?

Interview with Natalie Bennett

Jo Littler and Susanna Rustin interview the new leader of the Green Party.

Jo Green Party policies on the whole seem to be left-wing and anti-neoliberal: arguing for re-nationalising the railways, the social redistribution of wealth and a citizens' living wage, and arguing against economic growth as the best indicator of social progress. How are you going to let more people know about this, and how do you see the Greens operating in relation to a traditional 'left' terrain?

Natalie There's a huge political space in Britain for a progressive left-wing party that plans, for example, to re-nationalise the railways, make the minimum wage a living wage, build more affordable council housing, rein in the banks and rebuild Britain's manufacturing industries and food production. These are policies the Green Party has supported throughout its history. However there's currently so much significant political space available to us because the Labour Party has moved so far to the right. The Green Party now has a huge responsibility to make sure we communicate those policies effectively, and that process is happening. I see more and more Labour Party voters joining the Green Party when they see us in their area, and when they see that we are serious political contenders. People seem to have been waiting for us and are delighted we're here. So communication is essential: we have the policies, we've just got to get out there and make sure people know about them. To spread the word, we need growth, and the party is growing. We have core centres of influence and support in Brighton, Norwich, Lancaster and Oxford, and we need to expand from those centres and become a truly national party. Ultimately we want to be visible on all the national stages, and our next practical step in achieving this will be the county council elections in 2013, where we think we can significantly increase the number of Green Party councillors. Then in 2014 we think we can triple the number of Green Party MEPs, increasing the number to six (seven including Scotland). That will mean many more people voting Green at council and European level, so that by 2015 voting Green in a Westminster election will not look like a protest vote: it will just be taking advantage of the options available. It will be a case of voting Green and actually getting Green.

Jo What are you going to do to help the Green Party move beyond its traditional, safe, white, middle-class constituencies?

Natalie We are already demonstrating in certain areas - the West Midlands, for example - that we have moved beyond that demographic. In Solihull, we've gone up from zero to six councillors in two years - and Solihull is nothing like Brighton or Lancaster. We have also recently got our first councillor in Dudley, Will Duckworth, now deputy Green Party leader. We are focusing on issues like the living wage and speaking up for people with disabilities and their need for decent benefits. We want to insulate people's homes and make sure they can afford to pay their fuel bills. We're also aiming to secure Britain's food supply, and reduce the huge price hikes from so much imported food. All these are policies that should appeal in poorer areas. And in the last by-election in Highgate in Camden, for the first time we won the council estate part of the ward. In the past, I think the Green Party has sounded a bit technocratic. That's something we need to avoid now. I always try to talk in a way that is immediately comprehensible. And yes, the Green Party is relatively white, just like every other political party. That's definitely a problem. We have a new ethnic minorities network in the party working to try to improve this situation. The Green Party does not produce career politicians in the same way other parties do - if you want to be a career politician, you don't come to the Green Party! Instead, it produces committed people who really want to make a difference. So when those people get elected, they really do try to institute change. Voters are recognising this. Once they have elected one Green they are realising the benefits and electing more.

Jo How are you tackling the difficulties of making it onto the news agenda?

Natalie Let's pick one area: education. The Green Party has very distinctive policies

Green shoots?

here, and Labour tends to be quite conservative. For example we are the only party opposed to free schools, which are an outgrowth of Labour's academies. The Green Party has the policies, but we have not always done the best job of selling them. It should be easy to get media attention because we have distinctive things to say, but the reality is that when we are approached it usually has something to do with ice floes! We also really want to be talking about the privatisation of the NHS, re-nationalising the railways, and this huge range of issues that we have distinctive policies on.

Jo Is there enough mainstream media interest in environmental issues?

Natalie It's true that the media tends to be quite conservative on environmental issues, and doesn't take enough interest. In general there's an address book journalists have with a list of people they go to on education, on health or on other issues, and it's essential to be on that list. I was speaking to a journalist recently who said Green Party policies are too radical for people to be interested in them. Lots of journalists think people are only interested in policies that the *Daily Mail* will entertain. But the fact is that the public is looking for alternative answers. It is very clear that neoliberalism and globalisation have been an absolute disaster for the British economy and the world economy; for the British environment and the world environment. The media is doing a very poor job of giving people a menu of options to choose from. The options are out there. It's just very hard to get them any airtime.

Jo What relationship do the Greens have to the austerity agenda? There's been a lot of controversy in Brighton and Hove, for example, over the Green council implementing coalition cuts and sacking people.

Natalie When the Greens in Brighton and Hove set their first budget, they tried to implement the maximum 3.5 per cent council tax rise. This would have meant substantially fewer cuts. Unfortunately, because the Greens were only a minority administration, they didn't have the votes to carry the budget on their own. Labour sided with the Tories. Labour forced the cuts to happen because they *prevented* the council tax rise that would have raised enough money to make it possible to stop the cuts. So Green councillors in Brighton and Hove then had the

Soundings

options of either handing the budget over to the Tories, or of doing their utmost to produce the best possible budget. I'm confident that they did a good job of the latter. We tried very hard to not have a 'cuts budget' - cuts were minimal compared to what is happening in most places. The process itself was open and people were consulted and listened to, so that when cuts had to be made, Green councillors identified the best way to make them work.

Jo What will you be aiming for in terms of an alternative to the austerity agenda?

Natalie For the general election in 2010 we had our first fully-costed manifesto. That was a 'no cuts' manifesto, although there were some exceptions. We intended to cut Trident, nuclear weapons, road building, and to pull out of the war in Afghanistan. We had a programme based on the wealthy and multinational companies paying their fair share of tax. We rebalanced the tax system and ensured that we maintained benefit levels and maintained government services. The mathematics in that budget showed that this is perfectly possible to achieve. The current system reveals a huge tax deficit. As we've found with Starbucks, Google, Ikea and everyone else on that list, many companies aren't paying their taxes. That is why we have a budget problem.

Susanna Who are the MPs and other British politicians you most admire?

Natalie I admire Leanne Wood of Plaid Cymru, with whom I've shared platforms on several occasions. Plaid Cymru is a party we have much in common with, for example a belief in localism and local control. Leanne Wood is representing Wales on those issues, and trying to implement a very different kind of politics, one that's consensual. The culture of the Welsh Assembly also helps. Another politician I admire - although whose politics I perhaps have less in common with - is Alex Salmond. He has shown with the SNP how it's possible to go from being what is seen as a minority, special-interest fringe party to running a government.

Susanna If a future rainbow coalition government were to be formed, what would you, as Green leader, pick as your cabinet post, if you couldn't be Prime Minister or Chancellor?

Green shoots?

Natalie Green Party experience of coalition government around the world has not been encouraging. We would be more likely to look for a 'confidence and supply' arrangement in the event of a hung parliament. This is a system in which you negotiate your 'red lines' which the other party or parties must then agree to. It's hard to say now exactly what those issues would be; we'd certainly be thinking about Trident and nuclear power stations, but it'd depend what was on the table at the time. The Green Party would then ensure the government did not fall while remaining free to vote as our consciences dictated on particular bills. So a confidence and supply deal would be more important to us than cabinet positions. We're not after the chauffeur-driven car.

Jo How should the UK government be dealing with climate change?

Natalie The main requirement is a decent energy policy. Germany, for example, has announced that it will aim for its entire energy supply - not just power, but all energy - to be reliant on renewables by 2050. Britain needs to give industries more certainty about the future. The way to achieve this is through onshore and offshore wind farms, solar power, tidal power, and building a renewable energy policy that works. Such policies should secure our supply, help industry and provide lots of jobs. As the House of Lords recently identified, the government is also currently poor on energy conservation. Britain should be developing a decentralised, resilient grid relying on lots of small power sources from all over the country, with as many buildings as possible heading towards self-sufficiency. Kirklees council has just built a primary school that is sixty per cent energy self-sufficient; most of its energy is generated on-site. All buildings should be like that. The other aspect of a strong response to climate change is for Britain to stop declaring it can build an economy on financial services. We need to bring manufacturing and food production back to Britain. It is astonishing and disgraceful that only seven per cent of the food consumed in this country actually comes from here. To prepare for a low-carbon world we need to shorten our supply chains - particularly in food but also in clothing, furniture and other daily essentials. We need to greatly reduce carbon emissions by limiting the way we transport things around both the country and the world. Of course, that also means the end for the current model of extremely large supermarkets, which is entirely unsustainable.

Soundings

Susanna Does that amount to de-globalisation?

Natalie Yes. Although there will always be some things that it's necessary to produce at a global level. There will probably only ever be one global manufacturer of high-tech medical scanning machines, for example, and it might be that production of computers is limited to a small number of places, because of economies of scale and technical specialisation. However, it clearly doesn't make sense to grow carrots in Scotland, take them down to Cornwall and then drive them back to Scotland to be sold. This is the kind of madness that happens now. We have hollowed out our society while we have hollowed out our economy. If we have a few large multinational companies dealing exclusively with parts shipped in from China, these companies end up producing low-level retail jobs (usually poorly paid and not very interesting), plus a few driving jobs. A small number of high-level people will run this huge multinational corporation from the centre. There are no other jobs built around it: no technical jobs, no skilled jobs, no farm work. This predominance of multinational corporations means the risk of a jobless society. That doesn't make sense. You need strong local economies to create a range of work for everyone. The Bristol pound is a good example of something being done to improve this situation. If you have a local greengrocer who buys supplies from the farm just outside town, and the farmer employs an accountant just down the road, and the accountant employs a local builder - who in turn employs someone to look after their children - the pound that bought the first potato from the farmer circulates round and round in the local economy. That pound provides good quality jobs and social interactions between people who know and trust each other. This is a strong basis for society. It is the absolute opposite of the globalised situation that we have now.

Jo On a global level, the Greens hold positions of power in Brazil, France and Germany. That obviously has a lot to do with those countries' specific histories, but what do you think you can learn from Green parties across the globe?

Natalie The Green Party is the political wing of the green movement. Here, that green movement includes UK Uncut, Occupy, Transition Towns, Friends of the Earth, Greenpeace and similar groups. In the same way, we're part of the green movement globally, and a part of Green politics globally. Everyone in that movement

Green shoots?

has a shared understanding that we're currently living as though we had three planets when we've actually got one. The green movement is very clear on the fact that we have to move to a 'one planet' style of living very soon. We can learn from both the successes and mistakes of those other parties. One of the big differences between us and many continental Green parties is that they tend to be squeezed into certain political spaces as a consequence of proportional representation. There are many alternative left parties vying with the Greens for political space. When I go to Brussels and have meetings with European Greens, it's also evident that they think of us as much more radical than most European Green parties. So we do occupy a different political space because of different national politics; and we're less divided. That means that our Green Party contains many different strands that are often spread out over many parties in continental Europe.

Susanna The Green Party obviously favours a more pluralistic political system, with more smaller parties. Is there a danger with the weakness of the Lib Dems that Britain could move back to a two-party system and become more like the US?

Natalie I think it's true that the Lib Dems are going to disappear, with some local exceptions. But people's affiliation to all political parties has been diminishing over recent years at great speed. People no longer say 'I'm Tory' or 'I'm Labour till I die'. If we don't change the political system, we're going to see a lot more volatility. People are not necessarily going to vote Labour just because they always have. They may be prepared to vote for the independent candidate who will defend their NHS, for example. So, even with first-past-the-post we might start to get lots more different sorts of people and parties elected - though in a splintering effect - because people have had enough of almost indistinguishable Labour and Tory candidates. But it is also possible that because of disillusionment with the system turnout just gets lower and lower. That would be extremely dangerous. The democratic state depends upon consent and participation. People must vote. It is essential to acknowledge that politics is where decisions are made. Even if you go into the polling booth and write a rude word on the ballot paper, at least you're showing your dissatisfaction with the status quo.

Susanna If the Liberal Democrats do fade away and leave a vacuum as a consequence of their disastrous decision to join the coalition, might that not be quite dangerous?

Soundings

They have spent decades building up their political position. If that project fails could our democracy be damaged? Greens cannot just step in and fill the gap.

Natalie We can try! The problem with the Liberal Democrat project was that they didn't truly stand for anything except getting elected. There may have been a small number of civil liberties policies they stood for, but they quickly reneged on those. Economically, the Liberal Democrats stood for any policies or approach they thought would get them elected in a specific area. This means Liberal Democrats in different constituencies present different policies.

Susanna They stood for political reform, didn't they?

Natalie But they settled for an AV referendum, rather than insisting on a full PR referendum. If the latter had happened it would have been a very different beast to the referendum we actually had. I argued that people should vote yes in the referendum, but when I was asked why, all I could say was that it would be marginally better than the current system. As a way to sell change to people this was too limiting. I think a PR referendum could have been won but an AV referendum was never winnable. The Liberal Democrats' main mistake was not going into the coalition; it was their failure to insist on a PR referendum. As a consequence they have failed to deliver an entirely new politics at the next election. I've been uncomfortable with the Liberal Democrats for a long time, particularly at a local level. Obviously I'm not talking about every individual - of course there are good people in the Liberal Democrat Party. However in general my experience of the Lib Dems collectively in local politics was that they were frequently cynical, dishonest and untrustworthy. I might have voted Lib Dem before I became involved in politics and saw them in action. I would never have voted for them afterwards.

Susanna You have said you want the Greens to take over from the Liberal Democrats as Britain's third party. Does that mean that, like the Liberal Democrats, you'll be trying to win Tory votes?

Natalie Lots of people who vote Tory back many Green policies. One constituent in a Tory-dominated part of Chester recently commented that the Green leaflet was the

Green shoots?

first non-Tory political leaflet she had ever received. Conserving the environment, building up local economies, creating local jobs, insulating houses, reining in the banks, preventing mad financial speculation, reshaping Britain's economy to work for the people: many people who vote Tory are entirely comfortable with these suggestions. One thing I need to try to do as leader is not to use language that these people might instinctively be alienated by. We need to avoid the casual use of words that people react against. We can present our policies in ways that make clear they are relevant to people who would not normally identify themselves as 'left-wing'. Most people from both left and right would agree with reining in the banks - except for the one per cent of the population that is comprised of bankers. Everyone also recognises that it's essential to bring manufacturing and food production back to Britain. More and more people go into the supermarkets and see beans from Kenya and peas from Peru and realise that this is not a sustainable situation. There is huge public support for a plastic bag tax. Even some of what are considered to be our more radical policies are actually in line with public opinion. The idea of treating drugs as a health rather than a criminal issue, for example, is widely supported, to the point that Tories are now acknowledging that the war on drugs has failed.

Jo There's been a substantial expansion in green capitalism, and products and projects that use environmentalism as a branding tool whilst having an environmentally retrograde impact. How would you tackle this?

Natalie If the advert has a large flashing light stating how green the product is, it's time to start asking questions. But we are not trying to stop people from buying things. Instead we want to make the environmentally-friendly option the cheapest and easiest, so that it's the option people choose anyway. Ultimately, the Green Party is not about individual behaviour - but if we were running the government we would want those adverts to be absolutely honest. If we take transport as an example, the Greens would aim to make public transport cheaper than using your car. That way you don't have to force people to stop using their cars because the public transport option is cheap, regular and reliable enough. People would like their children to walk to school but at the moment, people feel roads are unsafe and feel forced to get into their cars. If you create a situation where the roads are safe enough, children could go back to walking to school. It's very hard for one individual parent to make a difference like this. Instead you need to change the whole society. We need to create a system in which laws, taxes, everything operates in a way that makes green the natural way to act. Then it won't just be about individual consumer decisions.

Susanna Looking ahead to 2015 and beyond, what are your feelings about what's happening within Labour? Are you optimistic that a Labour Party might emerge that the Greens can work with at some future date, given that a majority Green government is unlikely?

Natalie Sadly, all the signs suggest that until 2015 the Labour Party will hunker down, try to not say anything that offends anyone, try to not do anything that admits the mistakes they made while in government, and wait for the Tories to fall over and for the votes to fall into Labour's lap. They'll enter the 2015 election with a weak manifesto that aims to be all things to all people, does not stand for very much at all and certainly does not repudiate the worst mistakes of the Blair-Brown years. I'm not sure what will happen in that election, but the Greens would certainly not back a minority Tory administration. This means we would be left with Labour, and would have to find a way forward.

Susanna With the climate crisis so pressing, aren't environmentalists better served by lobbying existing politicians rather than supporting what remains a small party?

Natalie David Cameron and his friends have made clear that the lobbying model is dead. This is evident from what I have heard from Greenpeace and Friends of the Earth. People believed it was possible to lobby Labour, but Labour broadly failed on the environment - although their climate bill was good. The belief was that it would be possible to lobby this government too, especially when they put a green tree on their logo. However, lobbying has failed to deliver any amelioration in their climate-deadly policies. This means it's necessary to go into party politics. The evidence is very clear that lobbying by the green movement has failed as a tactic.

Susanna There is obviously a strong case in this country in favour of renewables. However, not everyone has our resources in terms of wind and sea, and the arguments around nuclear power are fiercely contested. Do you think there are

Green shoots?

issues in the broader green movement about evidence that need to be tackled?

Natalie The problem with foregrounding 'evidence-based policy' is that the other side can pull up some figures that suggest something different - figures that might not be reliable - and it becomes increasingly difficult for the ordinary person watching TV news to keep track. However, the fact that Germany - which has proved itself to be the state most competent at managing engineering, public administration and environmental organisation - is saying that its energy supply can be entirely based on renewables, and they want to be free from fossil fuels, is something to bear in mind. Another essential fact that doesn't get highlighted enough is that we know how much renewable energy sources are going to cost in the future. The wind, sun and tide will always be free. You can deliver dependable certainty with renewables which is entirely lacking with fossil fuels. Supposedly fixed prices of oil keep going up, gas is an unknowable quality, especially as the amount that fracking can produce in Britain is small, and relying on imported supplies raises serious questions.

Jo What's your opinion on direct action? Does it work?

Natalie The Green Party believes in non-violent direct action. As I had to say multiple times to a disbelieving ITV correspondent outside Hinckley Power Station (hoping she would ask her questions quickly, as I was sinking into some very deep mud), we are a political party and as such we believe in action through parliament. However, we also understand that direct action is essential in terms of piling on political pressure. If you go back through British political history, non-violent direct action has always been essential, particularly in terms of making the people in charge understand that things have to change.

This interview took place in London in November 2012.

Natalie Bennett is the leader of the Green Party of England and Wales. **Jo Littler** is a senior lecturer at City University and a member of the *Soundings* editorial board. **Susanna Rustin** is a journalist at *The Guardian*, a mum and a member of the Green Party

Why it's still kicking off everywhere

Paul Mason

Are we witnessing a global revolt against neoliberalism?

Two years on from the Arab Spring, I'm clearer about what it was that it inaugurated: it is a revolution. In some ways it parallels the revolutions of before - 1848, 1830, 1789 - and there are also echoes of the Prague spring, the US civil rights movement, the Russian 'mad summer of 1874' ... but in other ways it is unique. Above all, the relationship between the physical and the mental, the political and the cultural, seems to be inverted. There is a change in consciousness, the intuition that something big is possible, that a great change in the world's priorities is within people's grasp.

What is underpinning the unrest that has swept the globe? In reality it's reducible to three factors. Firstly, the neoliberal economic model has collapsed, and this has then been compounded by persistent attempts to go on making neoliberalism work: to ram the square peg into the round hole, thereby turning a slump into what looks like being a ten year global depression. Secondly there has been a revolution in technology that has made horizontal networks the default mode of activism and protest; this has destroyed the traditional means of disseminating ideology that persisted through two hundred years of industrial capitalism, and has made social media the irreversible norm. Thirdly, there has been a change in human consciousness: the emergence of what Manuel Castells calls 'the networked individual' - an expansion of the space and power of individual human beings and a change in the way they think; a change in the rate of change of ideas; an expansion of available knowledge; and a massive, almost unrecordable, revolution in culture.

Why it's still kicking off everywhere

What we are seeing is not the Arab Spring, the Russian Spring, the Maple Spring, Occupy, the *indignados*. We're seeing the Human Spring. We are seeing something that reminds us, long after the historians reduced it to a list of battles and constitutions, why they called 1848 the springtime of the nations; and why Hegel, in the aftermath of the first French revolution, wrote: 'Our epoch is a birth-time. The spirit of man has broken with the old order of things, and with the old ways of thinking, and is in the mind to let them all sink into the depths of the past and to set about its own transformation (*Phenomenology of Mind*, 1807)

The collapse of neoliberalism

As an economic model neoliberalism died on 15 September 2008. Alan Greenspan's words in the subsequent House Committee hearing were prophetic: 'I found a flaw', he said: 'A flaw in the model that I perceived [to be] ... a critical functioning structure that defines how the world works ... That's precisely the reason I was shocked, because I've been going for 40 years or more with very considerable evidence that it was working exceptionally well' (October 2008). Neoliberalism told us that the market was self-regulating; that the self-interest of the deal participant was a better policeman than the regulator. It created a dominant finance sector and told that sector to enrich itself - and that sector has now crashed the world economy.

We are left with what Nomura economist Richard Koo calls a 'balance sheet recession' - in which fiscal stimulus, zero interest rates and a $6 trillion global money printing operation can only keep the patient alive. The Western elite can't address this prolonged stagnation because it can't bear to do any of the things that would end the depression: write off the debts, inflate them away, or step back from globalisation to protect their own populations from its depressive effect on living standards. So they're left staring at the old model: and not only is the dynamo of it knackered, it is rapidly losing social legitimacy. All attempts to make the old model work without solving the global imbalances on which it rests lead to the policy of austerity: not just fiscal austerity, as in Britain and southern Europe, but a long-term strategy of reducing the wages, welfare benefits and labour rights of the workforce in the West.

And there is one massively important group that has been dealt not just a tactical setback but a strategic one. In *Why It's Kicking Off Everywhere* I called these

Soundings

'graduates without a future' - the first generation in the West since the 1930s who will be poorer than their parents.[1] They will leave college with £30, 40, 50k debts. The jobs on offer are - as the famous Santa Cruz 'Communiqué from an Absent Future' told us in 2009 - the same jobs you do while on campus: interning, barista, waiting tables, sex work. The first post-college job is often working for free or for the minimum wage. There is no way onto the housing ladder, the ladder is now horizontal; and in retirement, pension schemes will be gone.

You can add in further specific grievances, country by country: medieval attempts to roll back reproductive rights; endless small wars conducted against civilians; racism everywhere; torture as the default option not just in anti-terrorism but in the policing of minorities. In Europe there is relentless austerity - of the kind that forces you to eat or pay the rent. A whole generation is being forced to live as drifters - to relive the plots of 1930s movies: to get on a bus to look for work, to migrate, to sofa-surf, to enter relationships that are stark compromises between love and economics.

For this generation it is not a question of simple economic grievance but of the theft of the promised future. And I've become sick of hearing that the movement has 'petered out'. No. It has been massively repressed. Tear gas fired indiscriminately into crowds in Athens, rubber bullets in Madrid, tasers and pepper spray on campuses across America. Non-lethal policing is highly effective against non-violent protests. It tends to clear them away. But do not think it has cleared away the grievances in people's minds that led them to demonstrate in the first place. What it does is push those who don't want to get their heads broken into a more sullen, silent, passive resistance: a resistance of ideas; or a resistance of small, granular social projects; or, as in Greece, anomie - where people just embrace the beauty of being hopeless, roll a joint, stare into each other's eyes.

The crisis of neoliberalism, compounded by the total failure to emerge of any alternative within official politics, simply leaves unanswered the next generation's question: how does capitalism secure my future?

The revolution in technology

I recently rewatched the rushes my team shot on 15 September 2008 in New York City, the day Lehman Brothers collapsed. Two things struck me: the guys in the suits

Why it's still kicking off everywhere

don't realise how badly capitalism is about to come unstuck - and nor do I. Second, all the technology is, by now, obsolete. People on the sidewalk are filming the bankers on their Nokias, Motorolas, SonyEricssons - remember them? On that day Facebook had 100m users. It now has a billion. Twitter then had about 4m accounts worldwide. It now has 100 million. In the four years since the Lehman collapse the iPhone has conquered the world - and now Android. As for the plain old internet: 1.5bn people had it in September 2008, 2.4bn people have it now - that's 34 per cent of the world's population. But even that is an under-estimation: in Ethiopia, for example, there are twice as many Facebook accounts as there are internet connections.

The digital communications revolution is only one part of a wider technological revolution that has been under way since the middle of the 1990s, and has affected commerce (goodbye high streets), manufacturing (goodbye workers, hello robots), the speed of scientific discovery itself, and of course finance. But it turns out that the killer application of all these new technologies is to empower human beings: to think what they want, to act more autonomously, and to get knowledge they need. Clay Shirky summed up the effect of these technologies better and earlier than anybody: 'The current change, in one sentence, is this: most of the barriers to group action have collapsed and with those barriers we are free to explore new ways of gathering together and getting things done'.[2]

The effects of the communications revolution can be seen everywhere. In Egypt, the youth who took the decisive actions between December 2010 and February 2011 originally assembled as a loose affinity network using Facebook, around the *We Are All Khaled Sayeed* page. When the time came to act they were able to form up as small, quite distributed and horizontal groups: ten people on somebody's floor linked to another ten not by a command hierarchy but by trust, and numerous nodal connections. When they acted, they immediately began to use Facebook and Twitter to feed back information much faster than the security forces could; they bypassed the state media, which was paralysed, and when the internet was shut down they bypassed that too, using proxy servers and word of mouth: what they'd created on the internet they took out onto the streets.

Time and again over the past four years, beginning in Iran, the spontaneous defensive gesture that you see - replacing the clenched fist - is the phone raised to shoot video or take pictures. 'I'm recording you', it says. Of course the power

Soundings

of the gesture relies on international law, on an external media to publicise what's happening, but for me this is the new clenched fist of the twenty-first century. We saw it again recently in the March 2012 elections in Russia: when Putin's party was found to be perpetrating large-scale voter fraud, the proof, the outrage and then the call to action spread through social networks, which - because they overlap blogging sites, Twitter, Facebook and peer to peer information transfer - could not be shut down. Indeed I argue that they cannot even be adequately monitored or even recorded. This type of communication is horizontal, and it is networked. Spin and lies and inadvertent mistakes are easily challenged - and not just challenged but neutralised.

The type of action that grows out of such networked protest movements is completely different from that taken by Weberian hierarchal organisations: it is sporadic, voluntary, time limited. At the point you don't like it you break off; at the point it gets taken over, infiltrated, derailed, you stop and start again. Whereas with the labour movement you would never squander an organisation you'd spent years building, today movements like Climate Camp can just decide 'sod it, this is going nowhere'. And just as the movements are mercurial, so are the activists: they can pick and choose, they can have a day off; they can contribute a bit to each effort; they can meld their social life into their political efforts.

Castells captures perfectly what happened in 2011-12: 'By sharing sorrow and hope in the free public space of the Internet, by connecting to each other, and by envisioning projects from multiple sources of being, individuals formed networks, regardless of their personal views or organizational attachments. That is, they embarked on something that is the opposite of twentieth-century political practice: not parties, not campaigns, not united fronts, but sporadic swarms'. He continues: 'From the safety of cyberspace people from all ages and conditions moved towards occupying urban space, on a blind date with each other and with the destiny they wanted to forge'.[3]

I don't say that these movements are only horizontal networks. And in fact the actual moment of physical occupation of space was brief in most cases. In the US Zuccotti Square got cleared so thoroughly that even I, as a BBC reporter with a pass, was not allowed to stand there and report once it was empty. But a core of people have continued to flock to Tahrir Square over the last two years - that plebeian intersection between the Coptic TV actor, the secular leftist Arab, the football fans

Why it's still kicking off everywhere

and the educated young women. And Sol in Madrid was an incredible experience for those involved: 'You could almost taste the freedom', one of my colleagues in Spain said. While the time in Syntagma, in the summer of 2011, under the orange trees, with assemblies of 3000 going on amiably late into the night, modelled explicitly on the traditions of the *agora*, remains, for me, the high point of the Greek movement - before the descent into really cruel violence and the rise of fascism.

The big question of course is what all this leads to. Over time a critique of horizontalism has evolved. Long before Occupy, Malcolm Gladwell set the tone - networks are useful only for low-risk, low impact activism: 'The drawbacks of networks scarcely matter if the network isn't interested in systemic change - if it just wants to frighten or humiliate or make a splash - or if it doesn't need to think strategically. But if you're taking on a powerful and organized establishment you have to be a hierarchy'.[4] During the occupation of Zuccotti Park, Slavoj Zizek articulated a more nuanced criticism: the self-infatuation of the movements, the way they come to be about themselves: 'There is a danger. Don't fall in love with yourselves. We have a nice time here. But remember, carnivals come cheap. What matters is the day after, when we will have to return to normal lives. Will there be any changes then?'. Thomas Frank also criticised the lack of structure, the self-obsession, the lack of preparedness to embrace goals and demands, and the lack of connection with real life. He called for: 'a movement whose core values arise not from an abstract hostility to the state or from the need for protesters to find their voice, but rather from the everyday lives of working people'.

I think all these critics have something in common: they have lived through a time when structured, hierarchical movements with a clear counter-narrative and demands rose and fell. They understand the relationship between those kinds of movements and the old Fordist economy and the industrial working class. Equally, they all understand that the Fordist economy and the male, manual working class of the 1970s and 1980s has been destroyed and is not coming back. Mark Fisher, the inventor of the term 'capitalist realism', says: 'Although anarchist tactics are the most ineffective in attempting to defeat capital, capital has destroyed all the tactics that *were* effective, leaving this rump to propagate itself within the movement'. And what I think all the critics miss is the absolute congruence between modern work and this horizontalism, or networked organisation, with its weak ties, gestures, lack of achievements. Indeed I insist that horizontalism mirrors in great detail the way people exist at work, and the way they actually work. It is the new structure of the corporation that forces us to live these multiple lives: we are Paul in the suit at work; Paul in the combat trousers at night; Paul the Nord two-handed swordsman in Skyrim; Paul the Northern Soul obsessive on Tumblr. Corporate life forces us to have weak ties to our workmates, to constantly compete with them, to value social networking skills higher than actual skills: that's how you get a job of course - when many skills are quite easily learnable you have to be the person who can communicate and learn skills. Richard Sennett logged all these new attributes of modern work - weak ties, mercuriality, individualism - in his book *The New Culture of Capitalism*.[5] The revolts of 2010-11 have shown, quite simply, what this workforce looks like when it becomes collectively disillusioned, when it realises that the whole offer of self-betterment has been withdrawn.

I differ from these critics on a number of points. First, these movements are not trying to take power. They're trying - consciously or unconsciously - to form a counter-power within capitalism. It's a counter-power that rejects the conformist, stereotyped mass culture that the elite and the mainstream media are signed up to, but it is not yet prepared to offer an alternative. And there is a strategic reason for this: this generation has learned the lessons of the twentieth century. It has learned, as the communard Louise Michel once put it, that power monopolised is evil. It has grown up with Foucault, with Deleuze and Guattari, with the idea that the power relations inherent in hierarchical resistance movements are likely to lead, at best, to George Galloway, and at worst to Stalinism and Maoism. It has read Primo Levi, and it has read Vasily Grossmann.

On top of that - if they only knew it - these movements attempting to carve out alternative, more civilised, more self-controlled social spaces within capitalism are doing *exactly* what the pre-Leninist workers movement did. It annoys them when I say this, but they remind me of Edward Bernstein, the most centre-left of the German social democrats, who said 'the way is everything, the final goal nothing'. It really is not that far from that to the famous #OWS poster 'What is our one demand? Occupy Wall Street, 17 Sept 2011, Bring a Tent'.

Furthermore, there is no such thing any more as 'normal life' divorced from this experience of crisis and fragmentation. Those who think that by immersing themselves in the working men's club, or becoming an organiser for a trade union, the *indignados* would somehow be connecting to a reality that rectifies the

Why it's still kicking off everywhere

weaknesses of horizontalism are missing the point. And indeed former occupiers are now beginning to fan out into normal life - as seen for example in Occupy Sandy in New York, formed after the storms to help distribute relief; or perhaps more significantly, in Spain, where members of the M-15 movement have become - like the Russian Narodniks in 1874 - the organisers of hundreds of campaigns and squats in working-class communities. What they find there are poor, disenfranchised people - often highly articulate but shattered - in the same precarious position as them. Castells sums up a quite awful truth for those who wish the horizontalist movements would just wake up and return to the twentieth-century forms of structured politics: 'Networked social movements ... could not exist without the internet. But their significance is much deeper. They are suited for their role as agents of change in the network society, in sharp contrast with the obsolete political institutions inherited from a historically superseded social structure'.

The change in human consciousness

All this is connected to the third big factor that is driving change - a change in human behaviour, psychology and thought patterns. This is the least tangible factor, but I've come to the conclusion that it is probably the most important of the changes that underpin the unrest: it can survive quite a lot of reversals.

When the horizontalist movements arose, and the new culture around them - of raves, hip-hop, art activism, body art, sampling, photomontage, graphic novels - people immediately compared them to the 1960s. I argue that a more profound parallel is with the era before the First World War. That too was a period of rapid technological change, probably even more so than ours; and then, as now, the effect of many of the new technologies was to enhance personal freedom. In almost every novel of the time there's a liberated woman; and there's often an easily spottable gay man. And there's also a pervasive freedom, individualism.

It was Virginia Woolf who wrote 'on or about December 1910 human character changed'. What she meant was that new kinds of human being had been created by the combined impact of modernism in art and literature, suffragism and its allied women's social and sexual rights movements, mass consumption, and new technology. Stefan Zweig captured some of this in his memoir *The World of Yesterday*: 'There was more freedom and more beauty in the world ... in those ten years there

Soundings

was more freedom, informality and lack of inhibition than there had been in the entire preceding century'.[6]

How do the internet and social media and mobile comms change thinking and behaviour? I think they complete, and make irreversible, the small-scale social revolutions that started in the late 1960s: women's rights, gay rights, divorce, contraception, the human rights revolution in general. In the west, psychologists and sociologists documented the behaviour changes quite early on: Sherry Turkle, studying early computer gamers and bulletin board enthusiasts, noted the emergence of the so-called 'decentred self', that 'exists in many worlds and plays many roles at the same time' - and argued that people were using the internet as a 'social laboratory of the self'. Margaret Wertheim argued - and this was before Facebook, Twitter and even broadband - that we were using the internet to create a 'collective mental arena', where the act of sharing knowledge for free was causing the self to become 'leaky', 'joining each of us into a vast ocean, or web, of relationships with other leaky selves'.

In the 1990s, these early sociologists of Internet consciousness documented the behaviour patterns that are common now: swarming, multiple personalities, masquerading, stalking, community formation, intense personal relationships, seeing the online world as real, or hyper-real, and the constant attempts to create utopian communities. But they were writing the pre-history - because social media has brought these behaviours out of the world of the hidden, the online, the furtive parallel universe, and into the coffee bar, the living room, the university lecture theatre, the barricade, the tent camp.

There is of course a downside - or a claimed downside - to all this multi-tasking and hyper-social behaviour. For example there's a growing body of cognitive experiments that show that people fully immersed in the new technology perform worse on abstract thinking, on retaining facts, on inductive logic, on mindfulness etc.[7] And I'm prepared to accept that this is true. But here's one possible response to it: it's quite similar to what happened to physical skill when production moved from workshops to factories in the early nineteenth century. People who used to be able to make a Chippendale table now struggled to make a table leg. But if you measured the collective effort it was more efficient and collectively more intelligent. It is no surprise that the fragmented, de-centred, hyper-social self performs badly on tests designed in the Doris Day era.

Why it's still kicking off everywhere

All this is evidence that the cognitive, behavioural and psycho-social impacts of the communications revolution are real, rapid and unending. And above all they have created a zeitgeist - a series of signifiers that I think we're now in a position to understand: the V for Vendetta mask; the verbose sign written on cardboard; the chant 'Ash'ab nurid izqat al-nizam'; the acceptability of graffiti as both art and protest; the covering of people's bodies with tattoos and piercings; the ubiquity of graphic novels, of dance music; the white liquid Maalox which you put on your face against tear gas - and which the artist Molly Crabapple has now put onto the face of an oil painting. The most important thing about all these slogans, images and gestures is not what they say in isolation but what they express cumulatively.

And for me that is: scorn for the charade played out in the workplace, for discipline, hierarchy, targets achieved, the cheap business suit, the insincere smile, the dead language of corporate communications. And solidarity with one another - large parts of humanity signalling across borders and cultures their belief that a kinder, more human system is possible; and that it will be born out of the chaotic, ironic, playful qualities of human life - not by pitting one cruel hierarchy against another.

Where does it all go next?

We have to start by admitting that what is new in the situation does not abolish what is old. There are still unions, armies, Leninist groups with their perfectly preserved practice from the mid-1970s, hierarchical mainstream political parties and enough people coming out of university prepared to don a suit, look geeky, avoid drugs and, eventually, become special advisers, party staffers or MPs. And there are still workers, peasants and the bourgeoisie. So the classic revolutions - Egypt, Libya - and probably those still to come - Iran, Russia, China - will follow a modified form of the usual path: the eruption over democracy and human rights, then the move towards social justice and distribution, followed by splits in the movement and - finally - the question subsequently posed of whether the old power can come back in a new form: by force. This is the classic pattern established by 1848-51.

But here's the difference with 1848: by the mid-1850s capitalism was delivering - albeit under the guise of autocratic regimes in Europe - an upswing in living standards. Today, it is hard to see a long-term sustained global recovery; and in the west, unless there's a break with globalisation, social conditions are on a race if not to the bottom then to the point at which they meet the rising conditions of Asia and Latin America half way. It is therefore hard to see the upsurge of 2011-2 being followed by a long social peace such as we saw in the 1850s and 1860s.

In many ways 2012 was full of lessons to the pure horizontalist movement that politics abhors a vacuum, even one created for the best of intentions. As things turn nasty - for example with the attempt to roll back reproductive rights in America - it becomes clear that, although you can try to 'live despite capitalism', there are certain things you can't live despite: you can't live 'despite' fascist pogroms, you have to stop them; if you're a working-class young woman in America you can't live 'despite' the mass closure of contraception and abortion services. So people are propelled back into the structures, the system - to use it as a shield - even if they have no belief in that system. So the theatre group besieged by fascists in Athens, over the production of a gay themed play, demanded that the police protect them, and eventually they did - with tear gas. And Mitt Romney lost to Obama among women by a staggering 12 percentage points, largely because if you're a woman faced with a matter of fundamental rights, even if you're a horizontalist and dislike Obama's politics, or just cynical about the system in general, you're going to use your vote to protect yourself.

In the first four years after the crash of 1929, there was everywhere a swing to the right: austerity programmes, the rise of fascism, the self-marginalisation of the left. It was only in the face of the increasing threat from the far right later in the 1930s that the liberals and the left 'got real'. The rise of fascism propelled them from what Malcolm Gladwell might call low-risk activism to high-risk activism. As Castells points out, it is not hope that propels us to take high risks, but fear.

But the world that was created after 1945 - a world of human rights, democracy and relative working-class affluence in the West - is now in jeopardy. And as long as all these things remain in jeopardy, it will go on kicking off.

This is an edited and abridged version of the 2013 Amiel Trust lecture.

Notes

1. Paul Mason, *Why It's Kicking Off Everywhere*, Verso 2012.

Why it's still kicking off everywhere

2. Clay Shirky, *Here Comes Everybody*, Penguin 2008, chapter 1.

3. Manuel Castells, *Networks of Outrage and Hope, Social Movements in the Internet Age* Polity 2012, p2.

4. www.newyorker.com/reporting/2010/10/04/101004fa_fact_gladwell#ixzz2HWSnTC00.

5. Richard Sennett, *The New Culture of Capitalism*, Yale University Press 2006.

6. Stefan Zweig, *The World of Yesterday*, first published in Britain by Viking in 1943, p218.

7. See Nicholas Carr, 'Does the Internet Make You Dumber', *Wall Street Journal*, 5.6.10.

Railways - beyond privatisation

Paul Salveson

A strategy for bringing railways back into community control.

―――

Britain's railways have always been profoundly political. Ever since the inauspicious opening day of the Liverpool and Manchester Railway on 15 September 1830, when William Huskisson MP was mown down by Stephenson's *Rocket*, railways have had an uneasy relationship with politicians. And the question of ownership and co-ordination of the railways has always been a central area of dispute.

In 1997 the Blair government inherited a railway which had been privatised by John Major four years earlier, having made a commitment to creating a 'publicly-owned and publicly accountable railway'. This never happened, and for the last twenty years the structure inaugurated by Major has remained largely intact. During this period the cost of the railways to the state has nearly quadrupled - contrary to Tory claims that privatisation would reduce the costs of a bloated state-run bureaucracy. However the current franchised system hit the buffers in October 2012, when new secretary of state for transport Patrick McLoughlin announced the abandonment of the West Coast franchise and put a temporary halt to other bids. This article looks at past experiences of nationalisation and privatisation, and sets out a course for a new way to manage Britain's railways in a way that would meet the needs of both passengers and industry.

To start, we can take pride in the fact that Britain gave railways to the world. The astonishing talent of working-class Tynesider George Stephenson played a central

Railways - beyond privatisation

part in creating a national railway network that for many years was the envy of the rest of the world. By the 1860s, Britain had built a national railway network that had been entirely created by private capital. But the state made an intervention at an early stage with Gladstone's 1844 Railways Act, which subjected the railways to 'such conditions as are hereinafter contained for the benefit of the public', including cheap 'workmen's' fares; and this legislation started the long process of regulating railway safety, initially through the Board of Trade. However, for a long time nationalisation remained an unacceptable proposition, despite many of Europe's railways becoming state-owned by the end of the century.

One problem was the co-ordination of a national system. What emerged was a network of scores of private companies, each 'vertically integrated' with ownership of their own tracks and trains - though negotiated arrangements allowed for some degree of shared use of track. There was duplication and even triplication of routes as companies vied for their shares of the cake of Victorian economic prosperity. However, by the end of the nineteenth century the number of independent companies had reduced as the larger enterprises, such as the Great Western, Midland, London and North Western and North Eastern Railways swallowed up the smaller fish.

Towards the end of the nineteenth century the railways became a major focus for socialist and radical liberal attempts to tame unbridled capitalism. Critics of the railways pointed to excessive profits, a casual disregard for the safety of both passengers and employees, and the often inadequate standards of punctuality and comfort. Overcrowding on suburban services was rife, leading Lord Chief Justice Russell to comment in the 1890s that 'men, women and children are forced into trains in a way they would not herd sheep or bullocks'. This was grist to the mill for bodies such as the Railway Nationalisation League, formed in 1895; and the Independent Labour Party, formed in 1893, included railway nationalisation as a key objective. The railway trade unions had also become a force to be reckoned with by the turn of the century, and even the moderate Railway Clerks' Association called for public ownership, putting forward some creative ideas on ways of involving both workers and businesses in what we would now call a 'stakeholder board'.

The first world war placed huge burdens on the rail network, and the system was placed under temporary wartime government control. At the end of the war the newly reorganised Labour Party called for national ownership of railways and canals. But what instead happened was the amalgamation of the disparate

Soundings

collection of existing companies into 'The Big Four' - the Great Western, Southern, London Midland and London and North Eastern Railways. The 'railway interest' had successfully fought off widespread demands for outright state ownership, and, despite the nostalgic image of railways between the wars and 'the streamline age', the reality of the Big Four's stewardship of the railways in the interwar period was under-investment and cost-cutting. The huge burdens of the second world war brought the system to its knees and made nationalisation inevitable, almost regardless of who won the 1945 General Election.

But railway nationalisation was more than just a pragmatic move by the Attlee government. It was the culmination of decades of campaigning by socialists and railway trade unionists, and great hopes were placed on the new people's British Railways. Michael Young, writing in 1948, said that 'the nationalised industries should be models of industrial democracy which can later be followed elsewhere' (*Small Man - Big World*). However, the approach adopted for managing the railways and other newly-state owned industries was top-down and centralised, with more co-operative or democratic forms barely considered. Herbert Morrison had already developed ideas for the London Passenger Transport Board, set up to run transport in London, and this became the form adopted for other 'public corporations'. There was no room for passenger interests, or even those of employees, and the board was run by appointed 'experts'. This then became the model for the British Transport Commission, which was given overall charge of transport, and appointed a Railway Executive to run the trains. As a sop to the unions, Bill Allen of the locomotive drivers' union Aslef was given a place on the Executive's board. However most of the key jobs went to senior figures from the old private companies. Thus the opportunity to develop a more popular and accountable form of public ownership was missed.

The experience of the railways under public ownership was mixed. The desperate need for modernisation, after years of under-investment and war damage, was to some extent met by the 1955 Modernisation Plan, which inaugurated the replacement of steam traction by diesel and electric, and provided for serious investment in infrastructure. But the tide was running against rail transport, as car ownership began to grow. Some degree of rationalisation was inevitable, and it was also necessary to cut out some of the duplicated routes that were a legacy of the brief age of competition. But what actually happened was the appointment of Dr Richard Beeching as chairman of the British Railways Board (as the Railways Executive had been re-christened), with

Railways - beyond privatisation

a mandate to take an axe to much of the network, in order to achieve that increasingly impossible will o' the wisp, a profitable railway. His report, *The Re-shaping of British Railways*, published in 1963, was awesome in its implications, and left thousands of communities deprived of their railway services. Only a few of the threatened lines managed to survive the cull, and major routes fell victim, including 'the Waverley Line' that linked Carlisle and Edinburgh and served towns such as Hawick and Galashiels. The election of a Labour Government in 1964, with Barbara Castle as Minister of Transport, halted some of the closures, but most went ahead.

The closure programme had run its course by the early 1970s, but a new round of cuts was proposed under Margaret Thatcher in the early 1980s, in a report produced by Sir David Serpell. The Settle-Carlisle Line, which had managed to survive its threatened closure by Beeching, was once again proposed for abandonment. But the biggest campaign in railway history was mounted against the proposal, and in the end Conservative transport minister Michael Portillo bowed to the pressure and told BR to look instead at ways of developing the route. The fight for the Settle-Carlisle Line was the railway equivalent of the Miners' Strike. The campaigners' success in heading off closure made it difficult for either BR or the Thatcher government to contemplate further cuts in the network. The broadly-based campaign that had united Dales communities, trades unions and other supporters of the railway had paid off.

The BR that emerged in the late 1980s was increasingly at odds with the Thatcher government. A new breed of highly effective senior managers emerged who wanted to see an expanding, not contracting, railway. Management re-structuring led to a clearer focus on markets, with the emergence of InterCity, Network SouthEast (for the huge outer suburban network around London), and Provincial (later 'Regional Railways'). Each had talented managers who turned round the fortunes of a railway which had appeared to be in terminal decline. The British Railways Board was headed up by Bob Reid, who had the strength of character to take on the road-oriented civil servants in Whitehall - and by implication the Thatcher government itself.

As BR was renewing itself there was a parallel shift in local government. Barbara Castle had created passenger transport executives (PTEs) during her reign as transport minister in the late 1960s, and these had substantial powers to fund local passenger transport. The results started to become evident during the 1970s and early 1980s: Tyne and Wear got its Metro system, Greater Manchester began to develop a light rail network, and bus-rail interchanges were built at major centres in all of the PTE areas. Local rail services which had been threatened with closure in the Beeching report, such as the Leeds/ Ilkley/ Bradford/ Skipton network, were now electrified. Looking back on that time, many railway managers comment on how relatively easy and cost-effective it was to open new stations and introduce new services.

Despite the Thatcherite prejudice that state-run services were inefficient, by the late 1980s BR was probably the most efficient railway in Europe, working positively with the metropolitan PTEs to develop good quality local services, as well as investing in an InterCity network, which many continental railways rushed to copy. However, the tide was running against BR, and by the early 1990s various right-wing think-tanks were suggesting their favoured approach of privatisation. The John Major administration then bulldozed through the 1993 Railways Act, which ended the all-too-brief golden age of publicly-owned railways in the UK.

Rail privatisation: botched and bewildering

The structure that emerged after the 1993 Railways Act was based on the separation of operations and infrastructure, reflecting the neoliberal notion of 'freeing up' the railway network to the benefits of competition: a plethora of private operators could buy 'slots' to operate trains. However, there was a fundamental contradiction at the heart of the new system, given that passenger operations were in fact bundled up into more than twenty franchises, which were then put out to tender by the Office of Passenger Rail Franchising; only a small role was allotted to 'open access' companies, that of providing niche services that would be additional to the core franchised network. The first bids were won by a mixture of established private companies and some management teams, but the latter were quickly bought out by larger outfits. The establishment of the franchises in fact resulted in a network that was static, and dependent on state intervention for 'buying' in additional services. Far from freeing up entrepreneurial flair, the obstacles placed in front of potential open-access operators, particularly for the provision of passenger services, were immense; and open-access passenger services have never really taken off.

Freight was given a freer rein, with the former BR Railfreight business sold off

Railways - beyond privatisation

in chunks, and encouragement given to other private operators to enter the market. Like passenger services, these did not own their infrastructure, but, unlike most passenger services, they could operate as long-term businesses, and were not subject to the control of the Department for Transport.

Railtrack was set up as an infrastructure company, to own, manage and develop the railway infrastructure, and its main income stream was from track-access charges levied on train operators. This created a fairy-tale land in which Railtrack appeared to be a profitable enterprise - but with its profits based on government-subsidised franchisees paying a heavily loaded 'track-access' charge. However, in addition to track-access charges, which were fixed by state regulation, Railtrack also owned a vast property portfolio, which was potentially far more profitable than running a rail network. None of this was likely to lead to safe and efficient management, and the company also suffered a haemorrhage of talent, as experienced rail managers left the company, either for retirement or for more lucrative pastures as consultants. Routine maintenance, let alone investment, in the rail network suffered accordingly. The result was the Hatfield accident of October 2000, when a train derailed at high speed owing to corroded track. In the words of former head of the Strategic Rail Authority Sir Alistair Morton, the system suffered a 'collective nervous breakdown', which ultimately led to the intervention of the Blair government. A new body emerged for the ownership and maintenance of infrastructure, structured as a 'not-for-dividend' company - Network Rail. It fell short of the nationalisation that the rail unions demanded, but it at least took the railway infrastructure away from the short-termism of a profit-making business that was only accountable to its shareholders. However the basic structure of the industry remained intact, with franchising continuing for passenger operations, and the market being increasingly dominated by large groups such as First, Stagecoach and Go-Ahead. And a growing number of European state-owned railways, such as Netherlands Railways, German Rail and French operator SNCF began to win UK franchises, in some cases as joint ventures with UK-based private companies such as First and Serco.

The biggest winners from UK rail privatisation have been the banks. At privatisation, BR's rolling stock was sold off at bargain-basement prices to whoever was the highest bidder. But not many companies wanted to take the risk of bidding in what was then an uncertain market, and most bids were awarded to management buyout teams. However it turned out that the new rolling stock leasing companies proved to be very lucrative cash cows, and their new owners quickly sold up to various financial institutions - including HSBC. The rolling stock companies have subsequently enjoyed a period of massive profits in what is a protected market: nobody else has access to a large number of trains and the rolling stock companies can - and do - charge very high rates for leasing their trains to the franchised operators.

The basic structure that was created by the Major government in 1993 and survived the Blair years (apart from the re-structuring of Railtrack into Network Rail) has met few of the original objectives of rail privatisation. Costs to the state have almost quadrupled, and few passengers would say the service now provided by the private operators is better than what was delivered by BR. There has been a dramatic growth in passengers, but this is mainly because of external factors, including growing traffic congestion and the economic boom of the Blair/Brown years. Rail patronage tends to rise in parallel to economic growth (though growth has in fact continued in the last two years, albeit at a lower rate).

Britain's railways today

There's no doubt that passengers and staff (including many managers) are far from happy with the current structure and how it delivers. Fares are much higher than in other parts of Europe, while reliability compares poorly with some continental networks. And passengers are bewildered by the complexities of the privatised system.

Following the calamity of the Hatfield accident of 2000, the performance of Britain's railways is showing some steady improvement; more trains are running on time and a degree of confidence has returned to the system. Investment totalling over £9 billion announced by the Coalition government in summer 2012 will see many routes electrified and some lines re-opened. But it is at a cost. Apart from the government having to pump four times the amount of public money into the railways as it did in the last year of BR ownership, the cost today of doing things like opening new stations, providing new infrastructure or procuring rolling stock is also far greater than in pre-privatisation days. Part of this problem is caused by the large number of interfaces within the industry, with each component wanting its slice of the cake - adding profit onto profit. When the 2011 McNulty Review reported

Railways - beyond privatisation

on the potential 'savings' it had identified for the railways, this did not extend to any attempt to curb the super-profits made by the banks that own the rolling stock companies, or the plethora of other supplier organisations. And while the profits being made by the train operator owning groups are not so extreme as those of the rolling stock companies, nonetheless Northern Rail, for example, made £30 million last year, most of which went back to Serco shareholders and Dutch Railways: only about a tenth of that profit was invested back in the railway.

Devolution has made a difference to some parts of the system. Scotland has had rail re-openings, electrification and new trains. So has London. Even Wales, with a far less dense population, is seeing railways re-opened which would not stand a chance of getting approved in England. And in the North of England, passenger transport executives have seized the opportunity offered by the partial devolution of powers over rail to a subnational level: a new body - Rail in the North Executive - is emerging which may take on wide responsibilities including franchising powers (see below).

But many parts of the UK - particularly England outside of London - are stuck with an ageing fleet and serious overcrowding on many routes, and a lack of infrastructure capacity for the handling of any increase in traffic. The most urgent need is new rolling stock to extend existing train lengths, but this is immensely expensive given that most rolling stock companies are owned by the large banks. Investing in the infrastructure to allow more trains to run will take time, and this is what makes the most pressing issue now the provision of greater seat capacity.

A people's railway

A strategic national body

There is much that a centre-left government could do that would be electorally popular, deliver a better transport system, and save money. In particular there is a great need for a co-ordinated strategic vision for the UK's railways (this was to some extent provided for a short period by John Prescott's brainchild the Strategic Rail Authority, but it was abolished in 2006). A new strategic public body - National Rail - could give rail the sort of overall vision and direction it desperately needs.

Such a body would have different divisions that could operate with a degree of autonomy from the parent body. These could include infrastructure (Network Rail), Research (involving universities with specialist expertise), High-Speed Rail development, Rolling Stock, InterCity (currently 'Directly Operated Railways'), Freight Development, and Regional (which would operate with the involvement of devolved governments and authorities). The governance of National Rail should include a stakeholder board that gives a strong input to passengers, employees and the wider community. Via its InterCity UK division, National Rail would operate a strategic network of routes, but would leave regional services to devolved governments (Scotland, Wales and the English regions). It would manage existing franchises until they come up for renewal, but these would then be taken back into public control. National Rail would not operate freight services directly, but would encourage freight development through research, grants and infrastructure facilities.

Network Rail itself is already set up as a not-for-dividend company. However, it has little accountability either to government or the public - let alone its employees. Yet the current structure could relatively easily be transformed into a more accountable structure, which could then form the basis of a more strategic National Rail body. This approach would incentivise the staff, give them a real say in how the company is run, and ensure that senior managers and directors were accountable (and not being paid huge bonuses). It would ensure high standards of efficiency and bring more activities in-house, so that excess profits would no longer be being funnelled into sub-contractors' pockets. Surpluses, including those made from any savings, would go back into the railway to help deliver higher maintenance and safety standards.

The regional networks

The franchising system ushered in by the 1993 Railways Act has not worked. Costs have risen dramatically, and the collapse of the West Coast franchising process ought to be the final nail in its coffin. Franchising delivers a demoralised workforce, and employees who have little or no loyalty to what is likely to be a transient employer. Management is also demotivated, because franchise specifications leave little room for commercial initiative, and short-term franchises don't allow for investment by the franchisee unless specified in the contract.

Railways - beyond privatisation

It has been argued that if you get the franchise specification right, it doesn't matter who runs the trains, subject to appropriate safeguards. Yet there are a thousand and one issues which could never be enshrined in a contract which are absolutely critical to how a service is perceived by passengers, and what the company is like to work for. These are encapsulated in the notion of 'culture' - and creating one that combines entrepreneurial flair with social responsibility and excellent customer care. We need a new kind of rail operator that combines entrepreneurial initiative with an ethical approach, is founded on co-operative values, and recognises that there is more to the business than the financial bottom line. There must also be a social and environmental bottom line, which ought to be of equal importance. In fact many senior railway managers would welcome becoming part of a social enterprise, rather than having to work at the whim of faceless international groups whose only concern is narrow profit.

Regional franchises should be re-structured as licences, with new forms of accountability. They should be subject to periodic reviews, but not to compulsory re-tendering. If performance is good, why have to go through the turmoil and cost of a new competition? It's not good for passengers, for the employees, or for the wider public interest. This would allow for more long-term planning.

A 'social enterprise' train operator could be composed of several constituent bodies: employees need to have a stake, but so do passengers and other stakeholders such as local businesses. (Back in the early 1900s the Railway Clerks' Association (today's TSSA) argued for boards of socially-owned railway companies having chamber of commerce representation!)

On the more rural parts of the network, community rail partnerships have transformed the fortunes of many routes, but their capacity is now at the limit. A new approach to community railways is urgently needed, with devolved management and freedom to raise local funds to expand services and facilities. During the last twenty years some of the most successful private operators have been quite small (e.g. Chiltern, Merseyrail, Wessex Trains). Getting a mix of small, medium and even some larger-sized operations focused on distinct markets and regions is likely to deliver huge benefits.

We need to move on from franchising and encourage not-for-profit regional operators that are accountable to democratic devolved/regional bodies. An obvious place to start is Wales, which has a Labour government and a franchise that expires at 2018. (Ironically, it is currently operated by state-owned German Rail (DB) which owns Arriva, the franchisee.) When the franchise expires, the Welsh Assembly should set up a new body to run the railway network that would be accountable to local institutions and people. Another place where change could be brought about in the near future is Scotland. The ScotRail franchise will shortly come up for renewal, and the SNP government would like to explore the scope for a publicly-owned railway. The North of England is another area where there are huge opportunities, with a rail network that is desperately in need of investment, but subject to the whims of a London-centric Department for Transport.

The national and inter-regional network

If devolved agencies are best suited to co-ordinating local and regional services, the UK also needs a single 'InterCity' operation that connects all the main centres of the country. As noted above, we had this under BR and it worked: in fact many other European operators copied the idea, and you can see it today, operating superbly, in Germany, France, Sweden and many other parts of Europe.

There is already the basis to achieve this. The government has its own operation - Directly-Owned Railways - which is currently 'the operator of last resort'. At the moment it is already running East Coast - a major part of the national network. If it hadn't been politically embarrassing, it would also have taken on the West Coast line after the bidding fiasco, thereby effectively putting a majority of the main InterCity network in public ownership! However the government's current intention is to privatise East Coast when the current franchising mess is sorted out - if indeed it ever is. An incoming Labour government would have another option: to transform Directly-Owned Railways into a reconstituted 'InterCity' network, as part of the strategic body, National Rail.

It may well be that the West Coast shambles is still not resolved by 2015, meaning that it could easily be added to the InterCity UK portfolio owned by National Rail. The same could be done with Great Western, which is also due for renewal. That would leave in the private sector only the Midland Main Line (currently part of East Midlands franchise) and CrossCountry. These could also be taken into InterCity UK when those franchises expire.

Railways - beyond privatisation

Rail freight

Freight is a hugely important part of what rail can deliver. Currently there is a moratorium (and threat of abolition) on the Freight Facilities Grants that offered incentives for switching freight to rail. This 'cost-cutting' measure is a major backwards step, which will stymie future rail freight development. Though investment in infrastructure capacity will benefit freight as well as passenger operations, there also needs to be ongoing investment in depot and rolling stock resources - and without FFG that is far less likely.

Freight companies should be allowed to get on and win business, with support in the form of freight facilities grants, low track-access charges and other 'supply side' measures that could be delivered by National Rail. In the USA and Canada several short-line freight railroads are co-ops, and it would be good to see that evolve here, with government assistance. A future centre-left government could help freight, and indeed some secondary passenger operations, by establishing a social enterprise development agency (such as existed in the 1970s) with a remit to assist co-ops and social enterprises with expertise and soft loans or grants.

Conclusion

Any future incoming Labour government will be faced with acute financial constraints, and its policies will need to reflect that. But the suggestions made here would not be costly and can be implemented gradually - for example as franchises come up for renewal. The gradual absorption of franchises into InterCity UK, or as regionally-specified concessions, will actually be cheaper than the current costly franchising process, and they will deliver much greater benefit. Developing National Rail as a new strategic body - with the involvement both of UK and devolved governments, and of employee and passenger organisations - would not be a hugely expensive undertaking, while bringing more services in-house would help to control costs. Devolving routine maintenance to a more local level in some areas will also help reduce costs, as would using local skills for basic work (e.g. fencing, station maintenance, etc). If train operations became the responsibility of social enterprises we would see profits recycled back into the business, rather than being (literally in many cases) exported. But the biggest prize is rolling stock. Developing a strategy to take back rolling stock from the banks will not be easy, but if we are serious about bringing costs down and ensuring a supply of new trains to meet rising demand, it is a prize worth fighting for.

But the future of our railways is not simply a question of cost-cutting. What we need is an expanding railway - carrying more passengers and freight, and making a bigger contribution to sustainable economic regeneration.

Paul Salveson established and became general manager of the Association of Community Rail Partnerships, and went on to become a senior manager with Northern Rail, the UK's largest train operating company. He is a visiting professor at the University of Huddersfield and a local councillor in Kirklees, West Yorkshire. He is author of *Socialism with a Northern Accent* and (forthcoming in 2013) *Railpolitik: bringing railways back to the community*.

RAILPOLITIK

Bringing railways back to the community

Paul Salveson

New book from Paul Salveson to be published by Lawrence & Wishart in July 2013, discussing politics, ownership and railways. Combining historical analysis with personal experience and political theory, Salveson's research suggests an alternative ownership system for the rail networks and a possible future for Britain's transport system.

ISBN 9781907103810   £14.99
Also available on Kindle (ISBN 9781 907103 858)

Leveson and the prospects for media reform

Deborah Grayson and Des Freedman

Can the press barons be brought under control?

Just before the phone hacking crisis broke in July 2011, the Westminster Media Forum held a seminar on the prospects for future communications legislation. In a discussion focused on how best to deregulate the industry to ensure future growth, one audience member raised a question about whether legislation should include non-commercial priorities such as ethical considerations. This was met with stunned silence, followed by the dismissal of the idea by Google UK's public policy advisor as 'old-fashioned'.[1] Yet less than twenty-four hours later David Cameron had announced that there would be a full public inquiry into the practice, culture and ethics of the press.

This anecdote is a useful reminder of how far the conversation has come since summer 2011. Following the Leveson Inquiry and the four-volume report published in November 2012, there is no way that a focus on the ethical dimensions of news can now be dismissed as a thing of the past. Crucially, Leveson has provided a frame for discussing the behaviour of the press that the mainstream media has been unable to ignore. Stories that would otherwise have been interpreted as isolated incidents have been woven into a wider narrative about media power and responsibility, from the decision not to publish topless pictures of the Duchess of Cambridge to the long-awaited report repudiating the calumnies against the victims of the 1989 Hillsborough disaster.

Soundings

There is considerable evidence that the British public broadly accepts the need for tougher measures than either the press or politicians are willing to countenance. This support can be seen in strong polling for reforms - 79 per cent in favour of a regulator backed by statute and 76 per cent in favour of limits on media.[2] Strikingly, it can also be seen in the comment threads beneath articles on the *Daily Telegraph* and *Daily Mail* websites, many of which reject the editorial line that minor alterations to the status quo are an acceptable course of action.[3]

Events will have overtaken us by the time this article is published, but no doubt the central question will remain: is there the political courage in Westminster to side with the public against the unacceptable behaviour of media corporations, and to secure meaningful reforms to our media system that will change the way power is held to account?

What we learned from the inquiry

There can be no doubt that the Leveson Inquiry yielded a treasure trove of anecdotes, statistics and evidence about the often collusive partnerships between press, politicians and police. We found out that David Cameron found time to hold 1,404 meetings with 'media figures' while in opposition, one of which involved a personal visit to Rupert Murdoch in Santorini in order to 'build a relationship' with him. We learned of the countless texts between former News International CEO Rebekah Brooks and Cameron, many of which have yet to be made public. We discovered that there were 191 phone calls, 158 emails and 1,056 texts between News Corp and the Culture Secretary's office during its bid to take full control of BSkyB.

We heard from Sue Akers, former deputy assistant commissioner of the Metropolitan Police, that the *Sun* had set up a 'network of corrupted officials' and created a 'culture of illegal payments' in the police and other public services. We now know that there were 5,795 names in the notebook of the private investigator, Glenn Mulcaire, who worked for the *News of the World* and who was jailed for phone hacking in 2007.

It was, perhaps, inevitable that Lord Justice Leveson's recommendations would disappoint, given his extremely wide terms of reference. Even a year of hearings and a two-thousand-page report could only ever have scratched the surface of a remit

Leveson and the prospects for media reform

that stretched beyond phone hacking and press standards, into the murky world of the relationships between news organisations, police and politicians. The breadth of the inquiry undoubtedly lent it much of its power, and this in itself was a major coup for campaigners. But the wide nature of his brief also meant that the Lord Justice had to select from an enormous amount of potential material in order to produce a set of recommendations that had any hope of implementation.

Indeed, these terms of reference were constantly put under pressure. As Leveson himself remarked, there were 'no small number of people' prepared to criticise him for any suspected extension of his brief.[4] Thus, though the *Sun's* Page 3 clearly falls within the realms of press ethics, John Whittingdale, chair of the Culture, Media and Sport Select Committee, claimed that the judge had 'strayed' far beyond his remit by considering it.[5] Conversely, complaints that the report was doomed to irrelevance because it devoted only 12 pages to the internet were a smokescreen intended to undermine a proposed regulator.[6]

Yet there were significant exclusions, some of which could be seen at the outset in the denial to some of core participant status. Leveson clearly took pains to ensure that victims of press intrusion, particularly victims of crime, were at the centre of the inquiry. However disabled rights groups, for example, were refused core participant status, while groups seeking to highlight press Islamophobia felt compelled to set up an 'alternative' Leveson Inquiry after also being rejected. Such exclusions were early indications that Leveson was principally oriented towards the most direct and personalised forms of press abuse. While concern for these victims' welfare was undoubtedly sincere, this focus can also be seen as a calculated move to gear his recommendations towards the apparently 'achievable' task of designing a regulator to replace the discredited Press Complaints Commission - thereby sidelining issues of ownership, corruption and institutional failures.

This task was in itself a tall order, considering the competing interests involved. In one camp were the vast majority of the press editors and proprietors, willing to claim that their freedom was being curtailed at the slightest mention of any regulatory mechanism with teeth; in another we had politicians ever-conscious of a forthcoming election; while in a third were the victims of press abuse and their supporters in the general public, insistent on meaningful media reform for a more accountable press. Satisfying these often diametrically-opposed views required no small amount of clever manoeuvring - an artful balancing act with multiple tipping points.

Soundings

In these circumstances, it was to be expected that Leveson's recommendations - concerned above all with pragmatism and compromise - would propose a limited solution designed to deal with the immediate scandal of the consequences of press abuse, rather than with deeper concerns about a lack of media plurality and overly concentrated media ownership. And it was not surprising, either, that the government reacted to these rather consensual recommendations with disdain, while the press expressed outrage.

The report: cautious but welcome

Leveson's basic proposal was for the regulation of media ethics through voluntary membership of an independent regulatory structure, which would be based on incentives and overseen by a body recognised in law. These were remarkably similar to those recommended by the Media Reform Coalition.[7] Such plans would make a considerable difference to the practice of journalism in this country, particularly through the proposed arbitration service, which would in many cases operate as a low-cost alternative to the courts.

Leveson proposed that if a company or individual tried to muzzle the press by threatening libel action, they would first have to go through the arbitration service, which would then determine whether the story was in the public interest. Although such arbitration would not be compulsory, it would not be possible for anyone that bypassed the service and went straight to court to reclaim costs, and this would act as a strong inducement. The decision of the arbitrator could be taken into consideration in higher courts in any subsequent legal action. This would provide considerable protection for individual journalists and small publications, and it would also establish a channel of swift redress for ordinary people maligned by the press, who currently often wait years before taking the risky and expensive decision to sue.

This is why *Private Eye* has effectively shot itself in the foot in opposing any role for statute in regulation. An arbitration service of this sort could save news publications enormous amounts in court costs, but its decisions could only be recognised in higher courts if the arbitrator had legal underpinning. Laying aside the fact that the press is already subject to multiple forms of statute - from contempt of court to data protection - Leveson's proposals show that the right kind of

Leveson and the prospects for media reform

statutory backing could promote free speech rather than restricting it, especially for publications that excel at exposing and embarrassing powerful figures. A regulator backed by law is essential not only to prevent the slipping of standards that has happened after every previous attempt at self-regulation over the past seventy years, but also to establish an effective complaints mechanism that would protect both privacy *and* investigative journalism.

It was gratifying to hear Lord Justice Leveson trash the Press Complaints Commission's plan - led by Lords Hunt and Black - for a revamped self-regulatory system based on a series of commercial contracts. Leveson argued unequivocally that their proposal did not provide sufficient guarantees of independence from the industry, and did not 'come close' to what is needed to secure effective regulation.[8] However, despite this firm rejection of the industry's attempt to continue to mark its own homework, the consensus that has subsequently emerged between editors and senior Conservative politicians has been to develop a system - any system - that does not involve an auditor based in law.

At the time of writing there are a number of proposals on the table, including for a regulator governed by Royal Charter (proposed by Oliver Letwin, Conservative Minister of State for Policy), a revamped Press Complaints Commission (proposed by Lord Hunt in association with newspaper editors), and oversight by the Lord Chief Justice (suggested by the Labour Party). It remains to be seen which proposal prevails, and whether or not it fulfils Leveson's insistence that there must be some sort of legislation to 'underpin the independent self-regulatory system and facilitate its recognition in legal processes'. The outcome very much depends on the ability of campaigners to thwart the industry's moves to retain its overall control of self-regulatory structures.[9]

There are also some significant problems with some of Leveson's recommendations - for example the removal of journalists' privileges in relation to data, and the logging of all contacts between journalists and senior police officers. But a genuinely independent regulator, as laid down in his report, would be a welcome step towards a healthier relationship between the press and the general public.[10] In this context, David Cameron's refusal to implement what many see as entirely reasonable and proportionate measures is likely to reflect very badly on him. Yet, on its own, even a decent regulatory system would do little to address the institutional corruption between the media, police and politicians of all colours that prompted the inquiry, and which its testimony has underlined. And it is here that the Report's other shortcomings are evident.

The hearings certainly cracked the lid open on the private channels of communication between media executives and politicians and their special advisers, but Lord Leveson shied away from recommending any meaningful changes to address the profound threat to democracy posed by such political interference by the media in the political process. Tony Blair, himself under fire for maintaining excessively close relations with Rupert Murdoch, was unequivocal about the political impact of such relations:

> The media are obviously going to be a powerful part of society and in particular a powerful influence on political debate. Politicians will therefore interact with them closely ... This challenge is further complicated in respect of any individual political leader, by the fact that our views about particular media organisations are bound to be affected by how we are treated by them.[11]

However, despite hearing John Major's claim that Rupert Murdoch gave him an explicit ultimatum that his party would lose the support of the Murdoch newspapers if he didn't change government policy on Europe, Leveson found no evidence of a deal between the Conservatives and News Corporation over the BSkyB bid in 2011; nor did he find proof of an express 'deal' between Thatcher and Murdoch when the latter was allowed to take over the *Times* and *Sunday Times* in 1981. Yet the absence of a smoking gun should not be allowed to detract from the reams of other evidence of daily contacts between the culture department and corporate lobbyists - including, of course, the kind offer of Fred Michel, a senior News Corp lobbyist, to help draft a letter for George Osborne's office to speed up the proposed buyout of BSkyB.

Leveson also exonerated the former culture secretary Jeremy Hunt from accusations of lack of impartiality in his handling of the BSkyB bid, although he did reiterate that Hunt was responsible for the lapses of his special adviser Adam Smith, who, the report argued, should have been given more support and guidance to resist the 'intimacy, charm, volume and persistence' of approaches from Michel (Leveson Report, p1405). And this raises questions not only about Cameron's refusal to report Hunt for a clear breach of the Ministerial Code, but also about Leveson's reluctance

Leveson and the prospects for media reform

to firmly confront this serious issue.

Indeed the gap between policy problem and solution is nowhere more clear than in Leveson's lack of recommendations with regards to media mergers. Despite noting that a new approach was essential, and that 'repetition of the problems which arose in this [BSkyB] bid is undeniably not in the public interest' (Leveson Report, p1413), the report found that Hunt had no case to answer, and discretionary powers in respect of decisions over media mergers have been left with the secretary of state: while recognising a serious potential threat to democracy in the current approach, Leveson still backs the status quo.

The report's conclusions about the behaviour of the police were another major disappointment. It is true that, in order to avoid prejudicing upcoming trials Leveson was obliged to be circumspect about the inquiry's relationship to current police investigations into phone-hacking, computer hacking and bribery of officials. However, his statement when launching the report that he had 'seen no evidence that corruption by the press is a widespread problem in relation to the police' seemed to take little account of the incompleteness of the evidence he had heard, or the implications of some of the issues he touched on - such as the 1987 murder of private investigator Daniel Morgan.[12]

Morgan's case surfaced at the hearings in relation to the testimony of ex-Crimewatch presenter Jacqui Hames. She and her family were placed under comprehensive surveillance by the *News of the World* after fronting an appeal about the case on a Crimewatch edition in 2002. Her husband Dave Cook was at that time leading the fourth of five failed police investigations and prosecutions that have denied justice to the Morgan family for more than twenty-five years. The details of the Morgan case are complex, but what we do know is highly suggestive of widespread malpractice involving law enforcement and parts of the press.[13]

It was, perhaps, understandable that Leveson failed to tackle Morgan's murder head-on, since 'the issues arising would have taken weeks or months' of the Inquiry's time (Leveson Report, p24). And the report does make some recommendations in respect of press-police relations. But, as we have already noted, these are problematic. Restricting journalists' privileges in relation to data, and the logging of all contacts between journalists and senior police officers, are measures that are likely to further undermine the media's capacity to hold the police to account, whilst doing little to tackle the real roots of institutional corruption in cases such as these. A much more effective response would have been, firstly, to endorse the Morgan family's call for a judicial inquiry into the failed murder investigations (given the acknowledgement that due attention would have been beyond his own inquiry's resources); secondly, to recommend a public interest defence for journalists, recognised by the courts (as proposed by the Media Reform Coalition), which would make it harder, rather than easier, for corrupt elements within the police to sustain cover-ups; and finally - and crucially - to address the problem of concentrated media power.

What happened to ownership?

If Leveson was pragmatic and principled about self-regulation but cautious about the police and politicians, he was positively demure about wider structural questions. Underlying the hacking scandal and associated problems of press ethics is the issue of media ownership. The Media Reform Coalition has always argued that ownership lay well within Leveson's terms of reference, since he was required to make recommendations for a 'more effective policy and regulatory regime' to support (among other things) 'the plurality of the media'. Indeed, without addressing the problem of concentrated ownership there is little guarantee that we will ever secure a more ethical news media or a more diverse range of voices.

The phenomenon of press hacking arose out of a particular structural and institutional context, in corporations where decades of unchecked concentration of media power had created a culture of impunity stretching from boardrooms to newsrooms. In an era of long-term declines in circulation, hacking became a cheap means of filling column inches and scooping rival papers. And these same relentless pressures on resources have also acutely affected investigative and local journalism - areas that are central to the media's democratic role, where the response has generally been the disappearance of news desks, local offices and whole newspapers. Genuine solutions need to tackle this culture of impunity, but also to include measures to reverse the long-term decline in public interest journalism.

Although Leveson did not propose anything concrete with regards to ownership - preferring to hand the task back to parliament - three objectives were mapped out in his report. First, he argued that a new method is needed for measuring plurality, which would focus on the provision of news and current affairs and

Leveson and the prospects for media reform

include online publications. Secondly, he stated that triggers for intervention should be 'considerably lower' (p1470) than those appropriate to ordinary competition concerns, and should address organic growth within media markets as well as specific mergers and acquisitions. Thirdly, he suggested that a new system should accommodate a range of remedies and forms of intervention.

The proposals on plurality submitted by the Media Reform Coalition to the Leveson Inquiry directly and comprehensively address these areas. One key recommendation is for a 20 per cent limit on ownership within specific media markets (newspapers, radio, television, online), with a 15 per cent cap across the total media market (following a proposal made by Enders Analysis[14]). While these figures are necessarily somewhat arbitrary, they are based on the idea that the principle of fixed limits is essential in order to take the decision out of the hands of ministers, who are all too easily swayed by their personal relationships with media companies.[15] Companies which find themselves above the cap could go down the route of equity carve-out, selling a proportion of their shareholdings in order to bring themselves within the limit. This would avoid the potential danger of newspapers closing, and, in the current climate of shareholder activism, could lead to a genuine increase in internal plurality.

The Media Reform Coalition has also recommended the introduction of specific public interest obligations, which would be triggered when a company reaches 15 per cent of the audience within the media markets named above. These obligations would not involve the kinds of editorial standards imposed by public service regulation, but would be designed to promote a degree of *internal* pluralism, as well as a commitment to providing public interest news. For example, a public interest obligation to limit the absolute prerogative power of proprietors and senior management could be achieved by setting up an editorial panel that would include a number of staff journalists. This panel would not interfere in day-to-day editorial decisions, but could have powers such as that of proposing a motion of no confidence in an editor-in-chief, or hearing staff grievances.

The obligation to provide public interest news could be met in a variety of ways, either internally, by requiring minimal levels of investment in original news-gathering, or externally, through a levy on profits to support fledgling sectors of public interest journalism. Commercial press groups enjoy a significant public subsidy through VAT exemptions, and we believe it is entirely appropriate that the largest companies make a financial contribution towards areas that the market is failing to provide for. This money could fund entry-level journalism jobs or go towards non-profit news initiatives such as community radio, or could provide seed funding for co-operatives or foundation-supported models of investigative journalism.

These proposals are not unmindful of the high degree of volatility and uncertainty in the newspaper business, and the real prospect of some titles being sold or shut down. But such problems make the task of creating a diverse and accountable news media even more important, so that the fate of news outlets is not determined simply by the whims of proprietors and shareholders who have only a flimsy commitment to news as a vital democratic resource.

It is imperative that we do not allow the ownership question to be marginalised because of technicalities, or through a misplaced belief that the problem lies with individual journalists rather than with their thoroughly marketised work environment, which puts profit firmly before the public interest. Media concentration is notoriously difficult either to measure or remedy, but this is not a reason for abandoning policy altogether, and there are historical and contemporary precedents from which to draw ideas.[16]

Conclusion

It is entirely understandable that Lord Leveson felt that a clear focus on a new self-regulatory scheme was the best way to avoid his report gathering dust on academics' shelves, as has happened to the previous seven press inquiries. However, the fact that even his moderate proposals have faced such vigorous opposition demonstrates that such pragmatism is actually itself quite unrealistic. The editors' attempt to undermine the whole Leveson process is a perfect illustration of the continuing impact of press power. It makes little sense in this context to separate out questions of regulation and ownership.

We are unlikely to make significant progress towards a more democratic and accountable news media if we refuse to take decisive action to tackle its structure and to break up concentrations of media power. As well as challenging irresponsible and unethical journalism, we also need to focus on how best to stimulate good journalism through a range of incentives, ranging from new sources of funding and collaborative

Leveson and the prospects for media reform

news ventures, to the sorts of public interest obligations that we have outlined.

The polls we referred to earlier demonstrate that the public has little sympathy for attempts by corporate or political interests to dominate what should be *public* channels to inform democratic life. And the Leveson Inquiry highlighted just how distorted the relationships that mark our elite political culture have become; it showed that - as with the banks and parliament itself - these institutions lack legitimacy unless we can transform them to operate effectively in the public interest.

It is vital that we keep up our criticism of current attempts by both government and editors to water down Leveson's proposals. But it is just as crucial that this is accompanied by a determined attempt to change the shape, as well as the behaviour, of a news media that has all too often placed its own priorities far ahead of its responsibilities to its audience. This time, we hope, the public will not let the politicians off the hook or the press barons wriggle out of the mess they have created.

This article was written with advice from James Curran, Natalie Fenton, Angela Phillips and Justin Schlosberg.

Deborah Grayson is the campaign coordinator for the Media Reform Coalition, having previously worked for Yes to Fairer Votes and Climate Rush. She was ghost author of *Drugs Without the Hot Air* for Prof David Nutt (2012). She will begin a PhD in September 2013. **Des Freedman** is Reader in the Department of Media and Communications at Goldsmiths. He is author of *The Politics of Media Policy* (2008), and co-author (with James Curran and Natalie Fenton) of *Misunderstanding the Internet* (2012). He is chair of the Media Reform Coalition and a national council member of the Campaign for Press and Broadcasting Freedom.

Notes

1. See D. Freedman, 'Hackgate and the Communications Review: two separate planets?' openDemocracy, 11.7.11.

2. Media Standards Trust/YouGov poll November 2012: http://mediastandardstrust.org/mst-poll-results/; http://www.ippr.org/press-

releases/111/9185/more-than-three-quarters-of-public-want-strict-regulation-of-the-press-?megafilter=media; http://hackinginquiry.org/petition/.

3. For example, in response to J. Groves, 'Don't muzzle the Press: Culture Secretary voices her "grave concerns" over Leveson proposals', Mail Online, 1.12.12; and 'Leveson: key adviser warns compulsory press reform would be "illegal"', Telegraph Online, 2.12.12.

4. Quoted in J. Curran and A. Phillips, Evidence to the Leveson Inquiry, 13.7.12: www.levesoninquiry.org.uk/wp-content/uploads/2012/07/Transcript-of-Morning-Hearing-13-July-20121.pdf.

5. See BBC News, 'Leveson "strayed" far beyond his remit, Tory MP says', BBC News online, 13.9.12: www.bbc.co.uk/news/uk-politics-19583775.

6. See for example E. Bell, 'The Leveson inquiry is irrelevant to 21st-century journalism', *Guardian*, Comment Is Free, 28.11.12. Such criticisms ignore the continuing online dominance of existing newspapers and broadcasters, the potential applicability of Leveson's recommendations to large online news providers, and the absence, as yet, of any online-only publisher demonstrating anything like the institutional failings seen in the print media.

7. Media Reform Coalition, *Time for Media Reform: Proposals for a free and accountable media*, September 2012: www.mediareform.org.uk.

8. In his statement launching his report, 29.11.12: www.politicshome.com/uk/article/66965/lord_justice_levesons_statement_on_the_release_of_his_report.html.

9. Lord Justice Leveson, *An Inquiry into the Culture, Practices and Ethics of the Press*, Executive Summary, November 2012, p17: www.official-documents.gov.uk/document/hc1213/hc07/0779/0779.asp.

10. For some of the problems see V. Dodd, 'The Leveson report is a charter for control freaks in policing', *Comment is Free*, 17.12.12.

11. Tony Blair's written submission to the Leveson Inquiry: www.levesoninquiry.org.uk/wp-content/uploads/2012/05/Witness-Statement-of-Tony-Blair1.pdf.

12. For Leveson's launch statement see note 8.

13. See for example V. Dodd and S. Laville, 'Scotland Yard admits Daniel

Leveson and the prospects for media reform

Morgan's killers shielded by corruption', *Guardian*, 11.3.11.

14. See C. Enders' submission to the Leveson Inquiry, 9.7.12: www.levesoninquiry.org.uk/wp-content/uploads/2012/07/Submission-by-Claire-Enders-Enders-Analysis.pdf.

15. For more on this see *Time for Media Reform* (see note 7).

16. For recent developments on changes to media ownership in Argentina, see www.trust.org/trustmedia/news/argentina-new-law-will-benefit-media-pluralism-despite-polarized-climate/; see also the anti-concentration work of OpenMedia in Canada (www.openmedia.ca) and Free Press in the USA (http://www.freepress.net).

Revisiting the Olympic legacy

A roundtable discussion convened and organised by James Graham, with Bob Gilbert, Anna Minton, Mark Perryman, Gavin Poynter and Claire Westall

―――

One of the most important debates about the Games is the nature of their legacy. First of all let's look at the claim about their effects on increasing sporting participation.

Mark It's no surprise that soon after the Games athletics clubs in the East End of London were reporting hundreds of children turning up wanting to be Usain Bolt, wanting to be Jessica Ennis. The question is whether that will be sustained in eighteen months or two years time. There are huge question marks over that. There is absolutely no evidence from reports after previous Games that they have led to sustainable increases in participation in sport. And there is also no evidence for any connection between numbers of medals won and participation. For example Finland came sixtieth in the medals table at the 2012 Games, but they are number one in Europe for numbers of participation in sport. There are all kinds of different economic, social and cultural factors accounting for that. A very simple example of the disconnect between sporting success and mass participation is football. Once the Olympics were out of the way, sports pitches were full of football, the radio was full of football, the television was full of football, to the exclusion of almost any other sport. Does that lead, year on year, to increased participation in sport or in football? No. What the Olympics does is turn us into a world-leading spectator sport nation.

Claire. I don't think we'll see much change in sporting participation in schools - in terms of increased provision or the development of facilities - in the next five

Revisiting the Olympic legacy

years. This is already clear from education budgets and schools budgets, and the introduction of free schools will not help.

Does the left have a specific take on this?

Mark There is a broad consensus across the political parties on the Olympics and Paralympics. In the London mayoral election in 2012, the Olympic Games was the one issue that was not mentioned at all - because Boris Johnson and Ken Livingstone are in complete agreement on it. Both of them basically were saying, 'Come to London, and not only will we inspire a British generation to sport, but we will inspire the world'. There is a pomposity in these claims, right across the political spectrum. That means it is very difficult to use the usual terms of left and right on this - we are essentially a one-party state when it comes to the Olympic Games. And in fact, of course, if you simply discarded the entire discourse around legacy, the Olympics can appear to be a wonderful event. The day after the Games finished, everyone was saying that they did not care about the costs, that £318 per person was worth it because they had such a wonderful time. It could have been double that and it would still feel worth it. The disappointment comes in when you look at all those legacy claims - more jobs, the regeneration in East London, increased participation in sport. If you were not trying to make all those claims on behalf of the Games, if you discarded the entire discourse around legacy, you would then have much less of a problem around the Olympics.

One dominant narrative of the Olympics linked the whole faster, higher, stronger ethos to wider political claims. The Games were partly politicised through attempts by the government and others to claim this ethos for themselves, or for other areas of national life, including the economy. I wonder if we ever could appreciate the event purely as an event? But moving on to some of these other claims - that the Games would lead to jobs, to a better environment and so on - what is at stake here?

Anna One issue I would highlight here is the aim of 'convergence': that East London would reach a particular standard of living, improved healthcare, improved mortality rates, improved literacy - that it would begin to 'converge' with other areas when measured on these standards. But if we don't fundamentally look at the structures

Soundings

through which our society operates - including far more widely than East London - we are unlikely to be able to improve the huge social problems that exist there. The claim is that this work is already being done, but in fact this is far from the case. Convergence is one of the most pernicious claims, because it implies that the legacy organisers were looking at inequalities - but this is a complete misrepresentation. The Games were basically a huge development bonanza. And the original development model got completely out of control, with the taxpayer having to foot a £10 billion bill because the private sector could not/would not pay for it. We bailed out this project when really it could be seen as a high point within a failed economic mode - the one that has led to the financial crisis.

Gavin I think we all agree that the Olympics and Paralympics were great sporting events, which is one positive thing. And building cities and creating houses is potentially also a great thing. The problem comes when you put the two together. The narrative linking them has become something of a substitute for politics, as you get this consensus across the major parties and the way in which they perceive things. It seems that sport is the only way in which they feel that they can popularly legitimate any kind of investment. The legacy claims are very much associated with that path of legitimation. And of course you can achieve convergence - you can just move professional middle-class people into East London, and displace the people who currently live there. Then you get the required rise in living standards in East London so that it is comparable to the rest of the city. The astonishing range of promises that were made - on environmental sustainability, major housing development, the creation of new jobs - were all associated with a certain kind of economic model, as Anna says. And this model will tend to reinforce existing or past patterns of development, particularly in relation to employment. For example, if you take the Stratford Westfield Mall, most of the new jobs there are part-time and relatively insecure, and have many of the characteristics of the labour market that has existed for a long time for the poorer, long-term residents of East London. What appear to be rather progressive views about what kind of social transformation would be desirable, as stated in policies, actually often achieve quite regressive outcomes. And that has been underpinned by the coalition government's social policies that, in relation to housing and other welfare benefits, are tending to ensure the displacement of poorer residents further East, or somewhere else entirely - and this is already occurring. With a few notable exceptions there has not really been a challenge to this dominant discourse.

Revisiting the Olympic legacy

Presumably that is because the current buzz and the feelgood factor after the Olympics is just too valuable to those in power?

Gavin Absolutely. The rapid change in the values of politicians was really quite marked. Before the event, everything they said was about questions of security, transport and all of those nightmares and the concerns; there was a series of panics around these issues. That was quickly transformed after the success of the Games. Since then, opportunistic politicians have stepped in and said that we must capture this Olympic spirit and spread it in relation to developing our future and our policies towards a whole range of things. Some of the people that were involved with the whole event have been parachuted into government, and of course Boris Johnson - a classic example of an opportunistic politician - has been really trying to milk the Olympics.

Bob The legacy claims on environmental and ecological issues are also problematic, particularly around the site. I went to several events at the Olympic Park and there is no doubting that those grounds were stunningly done. They were a triumph of horticulture, they were beautifully laid out. And the effort of getting everything there to flower at the same time for twelve weeks of high summer, it was brilliant stuff! But if you start to make claims about that being environmentally or ecologically sound it becomes nonsense. It was really a form of wildlife gardening, of very high input and great intensity. If your aim was to genuinely promote biodiversity - which I think is one of the most important issues facing our species at the moment - then you have achieved the complete opposite. The site was originally Stratford marshland, tidal rivers and brownfield sites - and brownfield sites are among the most ecologically important sites in this country, home to 10 per cent of our rarest insects. But they didn't enhance these locations, they expunged them, replacing them with something completely different - an image of a bucolic countryside that never really existed. That is no model of sustainability. The iconic story that I love to tell about this is that Stratford used to have its own rarity, a plant called danewort, or the lesser elder, which is nationally scarce but used to grow in abundance in Stratford. In order to create this wildlife area, we dug that up and replaced it with what we determined a wildlife site should look like. So it is all a form of management. It was a beautiful site for the duration of the Games, but here too the legacy claims are contradictory.

Soundings

The Olympic Park - due to open in a couple of years' time - has been seen as an important part of the legacy, both socially and environmentally, and as a model for sustainable city development. What is your understanding of the Park as a sustainable endeavour, especially in its mixing of public and private?

Anna As has been the plan from the beginning, the Olympic Park is not really a public park at all. It was built on a Docklands type model, where every part of the Park, when completed, is sold off. The Olympic Village - the main development there so far - has already been sold off to the consortium owned by the Qatari royal family. It is now an entirely privately owned, privately controlled estate, within the park. And all the stadiums and individual venues will also be sold off for private ownership, private management. There was a case made in the run-up to the Games that the park should become a public park, managed by the Royal Parks, but that was blocked by the government, because it would not fit with their investment model of completing parts and gradually selling them off. And there is also an issue about whether the open spaces within the Olympic Park will be adopted by local authorities, or whether they too will just become parts of these private developments. That remains completely unclear. There is nothing at the moment to make me feel certain that it is going to be a genuinely public space in the way that Hampstead Heath is, or Richmond Park is.

Gavin Certainly since 2005, the public sector has paid all the money and taken all the risk. The private sector has stepped in only at points when there seemed to be a viable project to hand. The idea promoted by successive governments that the private sector will contribute to the public realm, or to urban infrastructure, is fanciful. In essence, the public sector creates the conditions for re-valorisation to take place, but it is the private sector which takes whatever value may arise in the future. In this sense, it should be noted, the Olympics has proved that the state plays a really important role in the relation to public investment in London. And this raises questions, or doubts, about using the word neoliberal to describe what's going on here. The state plays rather an important role in this sort of development (though, equally, it would be churlish not to recognise, for example, that Westfield shopping mall gets huge footfall and is very popular locally). However, there are no effective mechanisms in place to ensure that the value that might arise is distributed to existing residents or to socially disadvantaged working-class communities.

Revisiting the Olympic legacy

Mark Looking at the Park from the outside, through that huge fence, it does not look like a park. It is more like a very modern industrial estate. A long javelin's throw away from it you have Victoria Park, which is what I consider to be a park - a huge green space with a number of facilities, such as tennis courts, children's play areas, cricket nets, a few nice cafés, a couple of wildlife areas. That is what I think of as a park. That is what Green Park, St James's Park and others broadly look like. They are overwhelmingly green spaces. I just don't see what the Olympic Park will add up to as a space - though it may be that it will emerge as a useful economical unit.

Anna Another issue is that it has been modelled, from the very beginning, in relation to Westfield, who, among other things, wanted a dual carriageway running through the centre of the park in order to facilitate access to the shopping centre. As far as I know there are currently negotiations going on that suggest that it might not be a dual carriageway, but there will certainly be a main road cutting through the Park, going straight into the shopping centre and connecting it to motorways outside London. That is something that makes life very difficult for the legacy organisers.

Bob There is also the issue of the centralisation of park space. This is the creation of a very large, grand statement park. There is nothing wrong with that in principle, as with the Royal Parks. You could say that one of the great beauties of London is that huge expanse of large-scale parks throughout the centre of the city. However, what you are seeing with this centralisation of parks in Stratford is the focus of park space in one particular place, with the erosion of public open space throughout the surrounding area. This is reinforced by rising land values and the density of the development. Where I live, in Poplar, you see all sorts of little, casual open spaces used for development, while you have this one big central park space over in Stratford. There is a parallel here with the development of the big shopping centre and the concurrent loss of local shops. There is the one big open space or shopping centre that you make a trip to, that you drive to, that you spend half a day at, but there is a loss of that day-to-day contact that you get with the smaller green spaces and the smaller, independent shops. This is very noticeable with the erosion of garden space as we get more and more tower blocks. So the little spaces, such as the playground that you always go to on the way to or from school, or the green where the kids can run out and play football while you are doing the hoovering on a Saturday morning - these are

Soundings

the spaces that are being lost in favour of the grand statement.

What do you think will be the lasting effects of the opening and closing ceremonies, which were widely regarded as enchanting and inspiring?

Claire I was very surprised that so many people were enamoured of the opening ceremony, and that there were not more points of critique on Twitter or in other parts of the public domain - for example about the ways in which the 'Celtic Nations' were pushed to the periphery. The spectacle worked very well on television - the directorial tricks were amazing, with movement between live action and pre-recorded snippets and excerpts. However much of the politics was a message of union and cohesion, which seemed to override or simply bypass dissent or critique. Lots of historical moments were being aggrandised in ways that raised notable concern because the coming together they celebrated was based on historical amnesia. For example the Empire Windrush moment, the first major arrival of people from the Caribbean, was praised in the media, but actually, there had been no representation of the earlier imperial push outwards. It was as if these people arrived from nowhere and had no claim to be in Britain - which was certainly not the case. In general the glorifying of British multiculturalism was used to bypass questions of diversity that would be more controversial or challenging, and point to continuing inequalities. This was one of the threads that ran throughout the opening and the closing ceremonies. The idea of union and Britain as binding everyone together was an overt political message, and one that sought to obscure difference and inequality as well as their histories.

Anna But, for example, I was gobsmacked by seeing Doreen Lawrence and Shami Chakrabarti carrying the flag. I felt I had no criticisms there. That is how the coming together of the UK was symbolised for me. Of course the narrative was contradictory and it did not look at everything with the same weight. However, the dark satanic mills were given due consideration, which angered a lot of Tories.

Claire It did, but then the bucolic tree and the ecological greening of England came back again, after the satanic mills. There had been no enduring problem, no permanent destruction. I'm not expecting an opening ceremony to be a narrative of dissent, but what it did - in an interesting and very smart way - was show you

Revisiting the Olympic legacy

dissent without giving you the chance to attach yourself to it so that dissent was co-opted and never disruptive. It showed you dissent as a fleeting moment, so you could feel comfortable, but then it moved very quickly past it. I also felt that this all reflected where we are at the moment - in some positive ways, but mostly in negative ways. Which is to say that socially and culturally a narrative of progressive history won out, yet this was cast against economic crisis, debt and recession. That sums up the Olympics and Paralympics. Culturally, there was a narrative that Britain showed the world, about imagined equality, collectivity and success, but this was premised upon the unresolved inequalities - within Britain and across the world - that economically underpin the Olympics as one of capitalism's global mega-events

Anna But a few key moments of the opening ceremony could be described as healing - to use a word I do not usually feel comfortable with. Seeing Doreen Lawrence carrying the flag was quite an important moment. You can trace in that the legacy of the problems that this country has faced as a consequence of imperial expansion and immigration and subsequent difficulties. That was a patriotic moment, but not what one normally associated with that word.

Mark However, we cannot forget who the flag was then passed to - members of the armed forces. The militarisation of our national identity has seeped through into many different aspects of sport in this country, and that was very evident from the Games. The flag was carried to and run up the flagpole by members of the four armed forces, and throughout the Games, whenever somebody won a gold medal, the flag was again run up by members of the armed forces. And when the squaddies, the Paras, and the Royal Marines were doing their security duty in the East End, they were in the full camouflage uniform that they had been wearing in Afghanistan.

Claire The whole idea of Britain as a nation is problematic. The multi-nation state that is Britain is not really something British institutions want to deal with, and the Olympics allowed the message of Britishness to obscure political dissent - for example with the ongoing debates around Scottish potential independence. This dissent, and potentially the pulling apart of the Union, wasn't really a central ground for discussion at a sporting event, but it *was* central to many of the discursive messages that were being played out in the ceremonies and throughout the games.

Soundings

Mark Another thing that happened with the opening ceremony is that it became increasingly difficult to open up spaces of critique. While you might think that the Games were a fantastic event, you weren't able to say that it could be better. For example, there was such huge potential to maximise the numbers of people who could have been part of the Games, to spread the Olympics around the country, to increase the parts that were free to watch. Cycling is a good example here of a more democratic sport that takes place in public spaces. You do not need a stadium for a road race. I went to Teddington and Kingston to watch the road race, and it was done on the roads of Teddington and Kingston. There was nothing new put there for the purpose.

Bob That makes me think about the marathon and what happened with that - or rather what didn't happen. The decision was to stage the marathon *not* through the East End, but to transfer it to the West End, to the more photogenic, better off West End. It is an extremely rare event for the marathon not to end in the Stadium, and this seems to be a symbol of all the discussions we've had - about image, about narrative to the world, about London as an Olympic city, and ultimately about who the Olympics were for. The answer to the question of who is benefitting from the regeneration of the East End is prefigured in that decision about the marathon.

Mark It goes further than that because the marathon is usually an A to B route, so for 26.2 miles people can line that route in their hundreds of thousands - they do that every year during the London marathon. Instead, the Olympic marathon was run four times around a six-mile circuit. This dramatically cut the potential free audience, which was very significant considering there were relatively few free events at the Games. Look at the crowds that turned out for the cycling, that turned out for the triathlon - the potential audience was absolutely enormous.

Claire Instead of running though the East End they ran in circles that showed Landmark London to the world, a world full of potential tourists. And the decision to make sure that the televisual spectacle of the marathon would not show other spaces, spaces claimed as the heartlands of the games, undermined any claims being made about equality - whether economic equality, or equal opportunity for different parts of London to represent themselves. There wasn't even an opportunity for the East End to be seen by the world during the Olympics - the marathon underscored

Revisiting the Olympic legacy

the ways in which it was being erased in favour of the centre of British power.

Mark This was perhaps in pursuit of the most extraordinary legacy claim of the lot: that we needed the Games to promote London as a holiday destination, or even as a business destination. But why does London need any promoting? It is already a global business centre and the number one city tourist destination in the world, for goodness sake.

Anna And if we'd had a less glitzy, more democratic, sustainable and decentralised Games - which a lot of people wanted - we would still have had all of the wonderful moments the Olympics gave us. Those moments happened despite all of the crass commercialism and all the nonsense that we've been talking about.

Gavin The dominant story with legacy is that you use the Games as a spectacle to regenerate or develop part of a city. But in London's case it seems to have been the other way round - the narrative of regeneration served to reinforce London as a spectacle. Even those parts of East London that are being transformed, including some outside the immediate Park area, are being transformed to create expanded sales and events facilities - for example at Excel and the new Ikea site. You can see a certain kind of imagination being created - bits of East London that try to emulate the spectacle that is (or once was) the city. Challenging that is very important.

Jim Graham is Senior Lecturer in Media and Literary Studies at Middlesex University. **Bob Gilbert** is a longstanding campaigner and writer on the urban environment, and author of *The Green London Way* (L&W 2012). **Anna Minton** is a writer and journalist, and author of Ground Control (Penguin 2012): www.annaminton.com. **Mark Perryman** is a research fellow in sport and leisure culture at the University of Brighton, and author of *London 2012 How Was It For Us?* L&W June 2013. **Gavin Poynter** is Chair, London East Research Institute and Professor of Social Sciences, University of East London. **Claire Westall** is a Lecturer in the Department of English and Related Literature at the University of York. She is co-editor (with Michael Gardiner) of *Literature of an Independent England* (Palgrave 2013) and (with Rina Kim) of *Cross-Gendered Literary Voices* (Palgrave, 2012).

Journals from Lawrence and Wishart

Soundings

Soundings is one of the few places I know I will find serious radical thinking. Fearless, edgy and more necessary than ever

Suzanne Moore, Columnist, The Guardian

Individual issues £10, annual subscription £35 (three issues)

New Formations

New Formations is a genuine cultural theory journal, but one that at the same time incorporates the very best of the classical and the new in British cultural studies

Scott Lash

Individual issues £14.99, annual subscription £40 (three issues)

Renewal

Now we need Renewal more than ever to take forward a progressive agenda that engages with the big issues

David Miliband, MP

Individual issues £9.99/£14.99 (single/double issue)
Print-copy annual subscription £27.50 (four issues)
Electronic annual subscription £12.50 (four pdf issues)

Anarchist Studies

Many academic journals are interchangeable, but Anarchist Studies is full of material you will discover nowhere else

Colin Ward

Individual issues £10.99, annual subscription £20 (three issues)

Twentieth Century Communism

Twentieth Century Communism has quickly become an indispensable forum for those interested in communist history. It is fresh, lively, wide-ranging, and refreshingly free of polemics

Stuart Macintyre

Individual issues £25, annual subscription £25 (one issue)

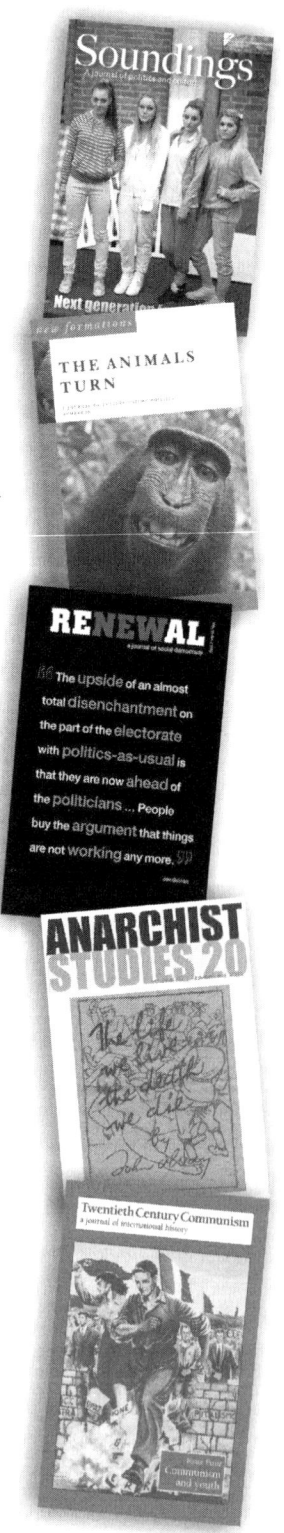

In France, will change be now or never?

Gavin Bowd

Can the Socialists achieve real change in France?

In May 1981 François Mitterrand became the first Socialist President of the French Fifth Republic. His two electoral slogans - 'Change Life' (inspired by vagabond poet Arthur Rimbaud) and 'Calm Strength' - managed to inspire hopes of radical change while allaying fears of Soviet tanks being parked beneath the Eiffel Tower. His triumph was followed a month later by a 'pink wave' that gave a thumping parliamentary majority to the Socialists. There then followed a modernising government that included ministers from a Communist Party that was already in sharp decline. But within three years, in the face of deep recession, the government had turned to monetarist 'rigour' and 'restructuring', while the Communists had returned to their shrinking ghetto.

In May 2012, François Hollande, one of Mitterrand's political children, managed at last to put a Socialist back in the Elysée Palace. His campaign slogan - 'Change is now' - appealed to those who had been sickened by Sarkozy's bling-bling style: according to satirical magazine *Le Canard enchaîné*, Sarkozy had tried to 'redecorate the Elysée palace in the colours of a Saint-Tropez discotheque'. And there were also Sarkozy's broken promises on spending power and jobs, and his inability to deal with the deepest recession since the war. Hollande presented himself as 'Monsieur Normal', seeming to break with both the vulgar excesses of the outgoing 'omnipresident' and the priapic outrages of the previous favourite for the Socialist candidacy, Dominique Strauss-Kahn.

Following the logic of the institutions of the French Republic, the dynamic in the subsequent parliamentary elections was towards the party of the elected

Soundings

President. The voters were both seduced and reassured by a government that pressed progressive buttons - a rise in the minimum wage, a return to retirement at sixty for certain categories, rent controls, requisition of empty properties for the homeless, a temporary super-tax of 75 per cent on the richest, a growth pact for the eurozone, tougher laws on sexual harassment, proposed legalisation of same-sex marriage - while avoiding the radical adventurism that might drag France further into the financial maelstrom. Hollande's party, of which he had been national secretary for many years, enjoyed a victory beyond its expectations: a clear majority for the Socialists and their allies. The greens would be included in the new coalition government, but there was no need to compromise with the Communist-dominated Left Front, which had been reduced to a mere ten seats from its previous total of nineteen.

At least in terms of electoral representation, France has never been so left-wing. The left has won the Presidency, the National Assembly and the Senate. Across the country it controls twenty-one out of twenty-two regions and six in ten departments. And yet the question inevitably arises of what change is truly possible now? What can all-conquering French social democracy meaningfully do in a European Union dominated by the right and in the grips of an international financial crisis? Does the new government in Paris offer an alternative to neoliberalism and austerity, or will it merely give a progressive patina to the European austerity measures being defended by Germany? The coming years will, in more ways than one, show what is left of the French Left.

Despite echoes of the early heady days of 1981, the picture for Socialist France is much more gloomy today. Whereas Mitterrand's Socialist-Communist coalition in its first years embarked on an exciting and markedly left-wing programme of reforms - including nationalisations, hikes in the minimum wage and benefits, new rights in the workplace, a reduction of the working week, the abolition of the death penalty and a rejuvenated Ministry of Culture - the present coalition moved to embrace 'rugged reality' after only three weeks. To the protests of the unions the minimum wage was increased by only 0.6 per cent - the equivalent of one baguette per week. At the same time, unemployment continued to increase, while official figures showed a large shortfall in public finances and predicted a sharp slowdown in what was already feeble economic growth. It is in such hostile conditions that the government, in accordance with the European Stability Pact, is seeking to reduce the

In France, will change be now or never?

deficit to 3 per cent by the end of 2013, and to achieve balance in 2017, an austerity plan that David Cameron has contrasted favourably with his own - but which the IMF and even the European Commission now consider unrealistically ambitious.[1]

To be fair, it could be argued that François Hollande is trying to play a particularly bad hand in the interests of progressive politics: if, in 1981, Mitterrand's *rupture avec le capitalisme* was out of sync with global recession and the onward march of monetarism, it could at least briefly thrive given that France that had a much smaller debt and, crucially, had control of its own currency. Today, France is saddled with a public debt at 90 per cent of GDP and must negotiate the perils of membership of the eurozone. Though the 'statist' tradition remains strong in France - with public spending amounting to 57 per cent of GDP - European laws on competition erect obstacles to any French government, left or right, that seeks to intervene in the economy to stop the loss of jobs.

Nevertheless, Francois Hollande's preference for 'solidarity' over 'austerity' initially appeared to pit him against German Chancellor Angela Merkel. In Hollande's ideal Europe, sovereign debt would be pooled, reducing its cost for poorer countries, while protectionist measures in favour of European manufacturers and bidders for public contracts would help create a bulwark against the worst ravages of globalisation. It was always hard to see 'Merkollande' succeeding 'Merkozy'. Even with the 'pinks' of Paris being liberated from Communist pressure, they seemed unlikely to embark on the kind of radical economic and social measures - liberalisation of the job market, cuts in unemployment benefit, pensions reform - that had been imposed a decade earlier by SPD leader Schroeder (which, though having some favourable impact on jobless figures, had served to alienate a significant chunk of the left's traditional support, notably the unions). The current Merkel-led push for tighter political and fiscal union goes against the grain with significant sections of the Socialist Party, particularly those loyal to the foreign minister Laurent Fabius. (In 2005 Fabius successfully campaigned against the European constitution; and at that time the French left decisively rejected what they saw as a fatal threat to national sovereignty and an enshrining of neoliberal economics.) And one further sign of Socialist steadfastness has been the new government's refusal to engage in the kind of stigmatisation of welfare 'scroungers' that has infected the Labour Party.

The new power in Paris could therefore be seen by many as offering an alternative to the austere, neoliberal 'disaster capitalism' being visited on the

Soundings

eurozone and elsewhere. But there are already signs that change may be never rather than now. Certainly at European level, the 'growth pact' - an injection of 120 billion euros into the European economy, half of which was simply unspent structural funds - represented only a very modest palliative to the Stability Pact, whose 'golden rule' on deficits has already sown disorder in the Paris coalition.

Some of the new government's symbolic changes could be understood as being indicative of its impotence - or at least of an emphasis on 'societal' measures rather than the addressing of urgent social problems. Thus it proudly boasts parity of men and women and a sprinkling of members of the 'visible minorities', but there is certainly no parity of social origins: the new ministers have all passed through top educational institutions and the Socialist or Green Party apparatuses; there is noone of working-class background, for example from the troubled Parisian suburbs, and no representation of the social movements and organisations that deal with the various problems that gnaw at France's social fabric. This contrasts with the coalition of 1981, which included Communists such as Marcel Rigout, the youngest of ten children, who had left school aged 12, and, as minister for youth training, was instrumental in creating hundreds of thousands of places for young people hitherto excluded from the education system.

The announcement by one of the fresh new faces, Najat Vallaud-Belkacem, Minister for Women's Rights, that she aimed to 'abolish' prostitution was very much in line with what appears to be a widespread form of magical political thinking - media-friendly, almost impossible to dislike, but ultimately unrealistic. Similarly, the new Minister of the Interior, Manuel Valls, ordered his police officers to cease using the familiar *tu* form during identity checks, but this hardly addresses the often execrable relations between the forces of law and order and those they claim to protect. Other incidents confirmed the old adage of '*plus ça change …*'. Thus, on one occasion, in the interests of Republican 'exemplarity' the 'normal' President chose to take the limousine rather than the plane, but his cortege was then caught speeding. The movie legend Gérard Depardieu's spectacular self-exile to the fiscal paradise of Belgium may have been denounced as 'pathetic' by prime minister Jan-Marc Ayrault, but it also attracted unwanted attention to the affair of a Swiss bank account allegedly once held by none other than the Minister for the Budget, Jerome Cahuzac.[2] In focusing on the symbolic there is always a danger of unintentionally bringing back into focus memories of the Socialists' own unhealthy and electorally

In France, will change be now or never?

fatal fascination with power and money in the 1980s, which was very much New Labour *avant la lettre*. And there was a further departure from republican norms during the parliamentary elections, when Hollande's current partner, Valérie Trierweiler, tweeted against his former partner Ségolène Royal - the kind of indiscretion that even Carla Bruni-Sarkozy had managed to avoid.

During his election campaign, Hollande declared 'my enemy is finance'. And on the question of intervening to help France's ailing industrial sector, he asked dramatically: 'Where is the State? Where is the President? Where is the Republic?' For some this may have revived hopes of Mitterrandist radicalism, but it became rapidly evident that what the Communists call 'the pedagogy of renunciation' in the face of all-conquering neoliberalism still dominates the 'modernised' thinking of the Socialist leadership. In 1981, the left coalition government intervened to prevent the privatisation of the SNCF rail network, while nationalising key sectors, notably in finance. And between 1997 and 2002, the 'plural left' coalition - which included Socialists, Communists and Greens - also intervened selectively to defend state-owned companies. But in 2012 the new coalition was much more timorous on the question of defending from closure the Mittal blast furnaces at Florange in Lorraine, the last steel-making plant in France. Top civil servants advised, in good French statist style, that a temporary nationalisation was perfectly legal and potentially lucrative, but the government did not act, for fear of raising hopes among other workers threatened with redundancy. The blast furnaces were closed, with consoling talk from government about help with the development of renewables. This 'betrayal' of the steel-workers of Lorraine echoed the reversals of the Mitterrand administration's 'modernisation' of industry in that part of France (which precipitated a doomed march on Paris and was followed by the departure of the Communist ministers from the government). After the capitulation at Florange, Hollande promised to do 'all he could' to save the Petroplus refinery in Normandy, but would not go further than offering the prospect of help from a public investment bank.

Despite promises of reform and economic growth within a couple of years, and talk of investment in green energy and the creative industries, the popularity of the Hollande government has collapsed more immediately and brutally than did that of Sarko. Official statistics implacably describe a mountain to climb: one in seven French citizens live in poverty, and unemployment is breaking the 10 per cent threshold (and affects 25 per cent of young people).

Soundings

Problems for the left

For hardened leftists, the 'social traitors' seem not to have changed their spots. But is there an alternative? During the presidential election, it appeared that the Left Front, with its charismatic presidential candidate Jean-Luc Mélenchon, was reviving the radical traditions that had taken such a battering since the 1980s. Gathering Communists, dissident socialists, Trotskyists, feminists and greens, this broad alliance - similar in some respects to Syriza in Greece - offered a programme putting 'the human first'. The Front's revivalist meetings, which cleverly reactivated memories of the French Revolution - the fall of the Bastille, Phrygian bonnets, Robespierre and Saint-Just - were among the highlights of what was generally considered to have been the best presidential campaign. And yet Mélenchon's score of 11 per cent, if very honourable compared with the Communist Marie-George Buffet's score of 2 per cent in 2005, was considerably less than had been hoped for - and was still way behind the 'disastrous' 15 per cent obtained by Georges Marchais in 1981. This disappointment was confirmed by the Front's 7 per cent at the parliamentary elections - which marked a modest advance, but was adversely affected by the lack of an electoral agreement with the Socialist Party, their traditional allies. The dynamism and visibility of the Front may have helped the Communist Party to pick itself up off the floor, but it still faces a Socialist steamroller. The 'Red Belt' around Paris, which once struck terror into the genteel *beaux quartiers* of the capital, is virtually no more. In an ironic twist of the dialectic, some of the best scores of the Front were in the heart of *la France profonde*, notably the Auvergne, where rural communism has resisted better the social changes of the last decades. The challenge to the Communists and the Left Front will be to articulate a credible left-wing programme that can challenge the ruling coalition and manage what the Reds themselves have singularly failed to do: retake bastions from the Pinks.

A special issue of *The Economist* recently claimed, not without reason, that, in France, 'the rich are routinely abused and people are instinctively hostile to capitalism';[3] but even the programme of the Left Front demonstrates the rightward shift of French politics. For the Front, the fundamental problem facing humanity remains total world domination by finance capital. But words such as 'capitalism' and 'class struggle' are virtually absent from its public statements: it is now imperative to 'block speculation' and 'detoxify' French businesses through

In France, will change be now or never?

the creation of a 'public financial pole'.[4] The socialisation of credit - rather than a clear break with the capitalist mode of production - is the order of the day, along with the promotion of 'eco-development'. In this, Jean-Luc Mélenchon remains fundamentally, but unavowedly, faithful to his mentor Mitterrand: this is radical reformism rather than red-blooded anti-capitalism.

But the course between pure oppositionalism and accommodation has always been a difficult one to steer. And, certainly, the first six months of the Hollande presidency gave ammunition to left-wing critics: Florange and Petroplus were not nationalised; employers were given 20 billion euros in tax breaks to aid competitiveness; and the 75 per cent super-tax was judged unconstitutional and seems to have been kicked into the long grass. But a realignment involving the left of the Socialist Party and its Green partners could lead to more concrete progress - and this prospect is already exacerbating tensions on the left between the recalcitrant Mélenchon and his more accommodating Communist allies. Traditionally, the Communists have not been classified as 'extreme left' because of their participation in government, at national and local level. But the current strident attacks on the 'fake' left in power are putting into question precious local alliances with the Socialists, and this could risk consigning the radical left to an even smaller and more impotent ghetto.

However, it is not simply the Socialist Party that threatens the radical left with oblivion. The left as a whole is facing the challenge of Marine Le Pen's resurgent National Front. The party appeared to suffer in 2007 as a result of Sarkozy's strategy of attracting their potential voters through a successful play upon the themes of immigration and law and order. However, when Sarkozy and the UMP once more adopted this hard-line approach in 2012, it had the effect of alienating their centrist voters while serving to 'de-demonise' the National Front, which duly welcomed back voters who had been disappointed by the Sarkozy government. Marine Le Pen's score of 17 per cent was in fact lower than the combined scores of her father and Bruno Mégret in 2002, but it nevertheless constituted a triumph for a party which had begun to be dismissed in the 1980s as a political phenomenon that would evaporate as quickly as Poujadism had done in the 1950s. The party has been consolidated under Marine Le Pen's charismatic leadership, and some of its more unsavoury elements have been, if not altogether eliminated then marginalised - including the Vichy nostalgics, SS pagan ritual enthusiasts, skinheads, and

Soundings

campaigners for a cathedral in Mecca. The discourse of the current National Front plays upon the precepts of the French Republic: an attachment to 'secularism' buttresses hostility to 'islamification', while defence of the 'French exception' justifies hearty renditions of the once-suspect *Marseillaise* at the end of party rallies.[5]

Although the Front's two parliamentary seats were won in its heartlands in the south of France, it also succeeded in spreading its electoral influence elsewhere, albeit not within the resolutely cosmopolitan Paris region. Le Pen lost by a whisker in the former mining town of Hénin-Beaumont, Pas-de-Calais; and the National Front has made progress throughout the 'rust belt', where both Socialists and Communists have failed to reproduce their traditional electorates. Eerily echoing Mélenchon (and even Marchais), the populist rhetoric of Le Pen denounces Hollande as being in the pocket of global finance: it is directing itself - more successfully - to the same electorate as the left, but through an articulation of fears about the immigration 'problem'. The crisis of the eurozone - which this Front wants to quit - threatens to create a perfect storm from which the far right will benefit.

Uncertain times

Recent works of literature have captured some of the strange and uncertain climate in contemporary France. In 2010 Michel Houellebecq won the Prix Goncourt with *The Map and the Territory*, which imagines the future of France as a post-industrial tourist paradise, offering the world an *art de vivre* of *hôtels de charme*, perfume and rabbit *rillettes*. And during the presidential campaign of 2012 Sabri Louatah's debut novel was a literary sensation; her *The Savages* imagines the assassination by a disaffected young immigrant of the first French President of Algerian descent. The candidate is a Socialist and his slogan is 'The future is now'. Both books ask questions about the troubled position of France, externally and internally. How can the country remain competitive and prosperous? Why are its high-tech innovations - the TGV fast trains, the Airbuses and proto-internet of Minitel - now fond but distant memories of the Mitterrand years? How can France respond to the restive youth of immigrant descent who were among the record numbers that did not vote for anyone in May and June 2012?

The 'sphinx' Francois Mitterrand liked to tell his protégés Hollande and

In France, will change be now or never?

Mélenchon that 'time should be left to run its course'. Indeed, the new Socialist president can console himself with the fact that, as even *The Economist* was forced to acknowledge, France remains the fifth-largest economy in the world, and the fourth-biggest recipient of foreign investment. What's more, the financial 'enemy' continues to lend France money at historically low rates. But the presidential mandate, now reduced to five years, gives less space than previously. In good social-democratic fashion, Hollande has let unions and employers negotiate the reform of the labour market. But if these negotiations fail, he will be faced with the option of following Schroeder in imposing 'flexibility' and facing down the protest on the streets. Hollande may have also created a hostage to fortune by promising that unemployment will begin to fall by the end of 2013, against all economic forecasts.

France is an impatient and gloomy country, whose quality of life does not prevent it from being Europe's biggest consumer of anti-depressants. François Hollande wants to be a normal President, but he - and French social democracy - may just not be made for these times.

Gavin Bowd is Senior Lecturer in French at the University of St Andrews. His publications include *Les guerres et les mots du general Paul Azan* and *La France et la Roumanie communiste*, both published by L'Harmattan.

Notes

1. See Angelique Chrisafis, 'Why Francois Hollande hopes David Cameron won't roll out the red carpet', *Guardian*, 9.7.12.

2. Cahuzac is accused of having had a private Swiss bank account for fifteen years. The Minister has publicly denied this, but - suspiciously - not filed a lawsuit. See Herve Martin, 'Cahuzac entre vaudeville et affaire d'Etat', *Le Canard enchaine*, 12.1212, p4.

3. 'So much to do, so little time', *Economist*, 17.11.12, p3.

4. See *L'Humain d'abord. Le programme du Front de Gauche et de son condidate commun Jean-Luc Melenchon*, Librio 2012.

5. The rise and evolution of the Front offer a striking illustration of what Nira Yuval-Davis described as the 'growth of the global phenomenon of autochthonic political projects' in the face of neoliberal globalisation and its discontents. Nira Yuval-Davis, 'The double crisis of governability and governmentality', *Soundings* 52, p88.

A connected society

Danielle Allen

Social connectedness has a key part to play
in the search for equality.

Political conditions in many countries presently demand that we undertake serious thinking all the way to the roots about how to build a progressive politics of egalitarian empowerment. In this essay I focus on the contribution that connectedness can make to such a politics. After discussing the relationship between egalitarian empowerment and social connectedness, I describe the economic, political and personal benefits that connectedness can bring, and reflect on how policy-makers could tackle the project of building a connected society.

Egalitarian empowerment, social structure and connectedness

If we are to work from the roots, I should start, briefly, with the original meaning of democracy. From the ancient Greek, of course, its literal meaning is 'people power', or - as one scholar has recently put it - the capacity on the part of a broad and inclusive public to effect change.[1] Insofar as the purpose of democracy is to empower individual citizens and give them sufficient control over their lives to protect themselves against domination, the core ideal of democracy is political equality.

What exactly is political equality? We have come to think of this ideal as consisting primarily of voting rights and the right to run for elected office. These political rights are, of course, fundamental, but this is a limited view. Voting rights are only one way to work toward the egalitarian empowerment of a citizenry. The achievement of freedom from domination depends on establishing something like a balance of powers among a multitude of particularistically interested individual

Soundings

citizens. The question is how to empower each and all within the competitive realm of politics such that none can dominate any of the others, nor any group dominate other citizens. This can be achieved only when there is broadly egalitarian economic empowerment, egalitarian educational empowerment and egalitarian social empowerment.

Yet political equality is not merely about empowering citizens across social classes and positions so that all are equipped to compete economically, educationally or socially with one another, and thereby to wrench balanced and fair outcomes from shared institutions. The best way to achieve freedom from domination for all citizens is to ensure that all participate through politics in creating those shared institutions in the first place. The goal is to engage a whole political community equally in the work of co-creating a shared public life.[2]

Thus the goal of political equality aims at two things: first, general egalitarian empowerment, and, second, broad participatory engagement of citizens in political life. And achieving these two goals requires paying attention to social structure.

What do I mean by social structure? I mean the very basic organisation of our lives through patterns of association: who do we know, who are our intimate associates, what organisations are we part of, who are the people to whom our connections are more distant but to whom we nonetheless have a connection? To which of our fellow citizens do we have no connection at all? One can imagine mapping one's own relationships. To make such a map is to capture one's associational life. The question of social structure is a matter of what this map looks like.[3]

Because economic life has so much power over our collective co-existence, the focus of progressive politics has long been on fiscal and monetary policy and how to redistribute the economic benefits of increases in national productivity. Yet fundamental features of social organisation themselves have equally profound economic and political consequences, and are equally important in the pursuit of egalitarian goals. Indeed, the failure to do right by social structure can have profoundly inegalitarian consequences.

Perhaps one of the most profound examples of a failure at the level of associational life in a democracy is the case of racial segregation in the US. And I am not referring here to a historical phenomenon, a relic that belongs in the mid-

A connected society

twentieth century. Racial segregation continues to have a significant impact on American life, and it has been pretty conclusively shown to be at the root of racial inequality along all dimensions: educational inequalities in terms of achievement gaps between white and African-American students; inequality in distribution of wealth; inequality in terms of employment mobility; inequality in terms of health.[4]

A study of segregation by a group of economists shows that social network effects have a great impact on the distribution of goods and resources, such that segregation can be a driver of group inequality, even in hypothetical, quantitative models, where groups begin with equivalent skill-sets and opportunities.[5]

Why does segregation have such profound effects? Common sense points the way to an explanation, which research has confirmed. All you have to do is think about what flows through social networks. At the most basic level, a human social network is like a web of streams and rivulets through which language flows. As language flows it carries with it knowledge and skills. That knowledge can be of the sort we recognise in schools: knowledge about the world or history or politics or literature. Or it can be of a practical kind: which jobs are about to become available because someone is retiring; the existence of a new factory that is about to be built, bringing new opportunities to an area. This sort of information also flows with language along social networks.

How did you get your current job? By virtue of reading a job advertisement? Or because you knew someone who knew someone who knew about an opportunity?

Any individual has access to just as much knowledge, skill and opportunity as his or her social network contains. And since knowledge, skill and opportunity are power, isolation in itself reduces resources of fundamental importance to egalitarian empowerment.

Language itself is one of the easiest markers to use in assessing how relatively well connected or fragmented any political community is.[6] Think of the power of dialect and accent in Britain; it speaks volumes - pardon the expression - about what a stratified society this has been.

I need to underscore that the point I am making here is not about race or ethnicity. It is about social experience for all people. Everyone is benefited by a rich social network and harmed by a relatively isolated or resource-impoverished social network. The American case of racial segregation just happens to be an extreme example of a basic phenomenon that crosses all contexts, times and places. More egalitarian societies, scholars have shown, are generally more connected societies, and connectivity is equalising.[7]

The benefits of connectedness

Now I need to say a little bit more about what I mean by connectivity, before going on to give a brief account of the egalitarian outcomes that flow from increased connectivity.

Social scientists have some technical vocabulary - some of which I'm sure you know - for describing what I have been calling connectivity. I will lay this vocabulary out here, and leave it to you to come up with politically more interesting ways of talking about these ideas. First of all, the benefits that flow from connectivity are generally called 'social capital'. By social capital, scholars mean the resources that individuals develop through their social networks, and the private and public payoffs that those networks bring.[8] Thus, learning about job opportunities can be seen as a private benefit. A public benefit would be the norms of reciprocity that develop in social networks, and make co-operation easier.

But what about the actual connections citizens have to one another? How should we think about them? Are there different kinds? Scholars of social capital distinguish among three kinds of social ties: bonding, bridging and linking. Bonding ties are those (generally strong) connections that bind kin, close friends and social similars to one another; bridging ties are those (generally weaker) ties that connect people across demographic cleavages (age, race, class, occupation, religion and the like); finally, linking ties are the vertical connections between people at different levels of a status hierarchy, as in, for instance, the employment context.[9]

Bridging ties are the hardest ones to come by. Bonding ties take care of themselves, really: they start with the family and radiate out. But bridging ties are a matter of social structure. Schools, the military, political bodies - these have typically been the institutions that bring people from different backgrounds together. A connected society is one that maximises active - in the sense of alive and engaged - bridging ties. This generally takes the work of institutions.

I noted a moment ago that more connected societies have been shown to

A connected society

be more egalitarian. In fact, I need to qualify that claim. It is more specifically societies that emphasise bridging ties - the ties that are harder to come by - that succeed along egalitarian dimensions. The problem with both segregation, in the extreme case, or fragmentation, in the common case, is an over-reliance on bonding ties: in the American case where white stays with white and black with black, and too few bridges are built, with devastating consequences for those on the losing end of that relationship.

The differences between these two categories of tie - bonding and bridging - do matter. Research shows, for instance, that the majority of people who get a new job through information passed through a social network have acquired that information not from a close connection but from a distant one.[10] This makes sense. One's closest connections share too much of one's world; they are a lot less likely to introduce new information.

We all know this intuitively. Thus, for example, when we're trying to help a friend who has been single too long we scratch our brains to think of a further removed social connection who might connect our friend to a whole new pool of possibilities. That may seem like a trivial example, but the most important egalitarian impacts of social connectivity flow from bridging ties and their impact on the diffusion of knowledge. Many economic, political and personal benefits flow from bridging ties. There is not space here to give a full account of all of these benefits, so I will simply list them briefly and give references for those interested in further detail.

For the economy, one benefit of a connected society is improvements in education - because connectedness enables a broader diffusion of the linguistic, intellectual and social resources that support learning in the first place, and has an impact on personal decisions about whether to invest in education. A further benefit is increased social mobility - because a better diffusion of information allows people to see opportunities and fit themselves to them. Connectedness also increases creativity - because diverse approaches to problem solving are more likely to be brought into conversation with one another; and it brings about more efficient knowledge transmission - because information travels faster across bridging connections.[11]

For democratic politics, the benefits of a connected society include: improved social awareness and public discourse - because citizens have more exposure to the impacts on others of different policy questions, and because improved information-flows across social ties mean that citizens are less likely to consider the beliefs of others to be simply incorrect; more efficient policy-planning - because policy-makers can more easily draw on local knowledge to ensure alignment of policies with on-the-ground realities; and the bringing into being of what were previously only 'latent publics' - because social connections across communities help communities discover new kinds of alliances.[12] Furthermore, a background cultural expectation of connectedness serves to set into even sharper relief 'disconnected', 'out-of-touch' policy approaches - such as that of the Tories when they developed NHS reform without consultation with the holders of local knowledge.

For personal well-being, the benefits of a connected society include: an increased sense of agency because of access to a larger opportunity network; increased opportunity to develop important relational skills - not merely those that support the intimacy of bonding relations, but also the skills of the interpreter, mediator and greeter, which serve to build and use bridging relationships; and the opportunity to protect and enjoy one's own culture without falling into isolation.[13]

And one final - and crucial - benefit of a connected society is that it offers an alternative way of thinking about belonging and integration. For the sake of healthy psychological development, all people need bonding relationships, intimate relationships with people who are like ourselves.[14] But too often the effort to combat social isolation has focused on an ideal of integration that has collapsed into a project of assimilation, where the goal is to make sure that the alienated and isolated learn how to be like those who have the upper hand economically, politically and socially.[15] The alienated and isolated are told, in other words, that in order to achieve economic, political and social empowerment, they have to give up some important element out of which they are made. This does harm to individual identities. For this reason, we can and should put aside the language of integration and assimilation. And here the goal of connectivity provides an alternative.

Achieving a connected society does not require that individuals shed cultural specificity. Instead it requires that we scrutinise how institutions build social connections with a view to ensuring that there are multiple, overlapping, pathways connecting the full range of communities in a country to one another. The ideal of a connected society contrasts to an idea of integration-through-assimilation by orienting us toward becoming a community of communities. A connected society

A connected society

respects and protects bonding ties while also maximising bridging ties.

To summarise the argument so far: a commitment to democracy requires the ideal of political equality; and the ideal of political equality requires the pursuit of a broadly egalitarian empowerment of citizens along economic, political and social dimensions; and within this, far more attention needs to be given to just how powerful social structure is (in particular in patterns of bonding and bridging social ties) in causing egalitarian or inegalitarian outcomes; there is thus a need for building a connected society that maximises bridging ties, and develops means whereby such ties can support egalitarian empowerment.

I would like now to explore how these arguments might help to address some questions of policy in the specific context of the Labour Party's policy review in the UK. What policy frameworks would support building a connected society, within a project of broad egalitarian empowerment?

One nation as a connected nation

The Labour Party has recently been asking what it would mean for Labour to lead an initiative to build a 'One Nation' culture. This is a conversation about ideals. Labour is trying to define what the democratic people of the United Kingdom stands for.

I would argue that Labour's 'One Nation' should also be 'A Connected Nation'.

How does one build a connected nation? One pursues active connections, interweaving all of the many communities out of which the whole community is made. Below I briefly mention some important areas where this kind of work could be done.

One of Labour's current policies is to pursue apprenticeship programmes. One third of major companies now have them, and that number should, of course, be pushed up. But my argument is that those apprentice programmes should also be 'Connector' programmes. How well are the companies and institutions that run apprentice programmes tapping into diverse communities? How well do they support apprentices in forming links with one another across social divides? How often are the linking connections between those who employ apprentices and the apprentices themselves used to generate 'reverse mentorships', whereby the employers can learn something more about the world from which the apprentices come?

Soundings

A focus on connectedness could also involve exploring how major institutions - not only corporations but also universities and churches - could play a greater role as social connectors. Take universities as an example. At Lehigh University in Pennsylvania, some very active faculty members realised that members of a local community suffering from severe unemployment and environmental issues like asthma needed the kind of knowledge that was circulating inside the walls of the university mere blocks away. Those faculty members have subsequently worked to build programmes to connect the knowledge resources of the university and the community, and have made those programmes the basis of new local policy-making initiatives.[16]

A further area of exploration might be to ask whether policy-making could be connected to grass-roots story-telling. In the US context, the 2008 Obama for America campaign used the strategies of urban organisers to connect a lot of people - from across classes, and both in person and online - to a shared project of identifying what was wrong with the contemporary American situation. This typically involved asking a lot of people who didn't know each other to begin a conversation by telling their stories. But these stories ultimately provided the basis of the highly detailed picture of the healthcare situation in the US that led to the creation and passage of the Affordable Care Act - and, happily, in the 2012 election, to its reaffirmation. I don't think any of this would have happened without the analytical specificity that was made possible by asking a lot of ordinary people from all over the country to connect with each other by telling their stories about an important issue.

Another example is housing policy. Under the Coalition government the trend has been towards a greater segregation of housing by income. What is Labour's policy on mixed-income housing? Research indicates that that low-income families who move out of neighbourhoods of concentrated poverty into mixed-income neighbourhoods fare better. Can mixed income housing be protected? Failure on this point is one of the greatest afflictions of the American situation.

And then there is transportation. This is not merely an economic issue; it is also at the core of this subject of connectedness. To the degree that the public transport system has ceased to support the British public in pursuing its goals for mobility, it stands in the way of the achievement of a connected society.

A connected society

As we have seen, education is an important domain for thinking about building a connected society. Can we build common schools that genuinely bring together students from different communities? Can exclusive, elite schools learn to open themselves up more broadly or develop true partnerships with schools that are very different from themselves?

Finally, there is this simple thing. Every social gathering is an opportunity to build human networks in new ways. Who is not here at today's meeting? Who should be here? Are there representatives from places and contexts who could function as valuable connectors, helping to build new bridging ties, who might be invited to this conversation and others like it?

One has to ask that question constantly; one has to encourage the leaders of all major institutions to ask it. That too is part of the slow, person-to-person level work involved in building a connected society.

On the basis of increased connectivity, though, individuals can be empowered and, on the basis of that empowerment, the broader phenomenon, 'people power', can come slowly and with labour into existence.

This article is an edited version of a talk at the seminar 'Why One Nation Labour needs a connected society', 27.11.12, organised by the Labour Party Policy Review in association with Demos.

Danielle Allen is UPS Foundation Professor of Social Sciences at the Institute for Advanced Study in Princeton, NJ. She is author, among other books, of *Talking to Strangers: anxieties of citizenship since Brown v. Board of Education* (Chicago 2004) and *Why the Declaration of Independence Matters* (Norton/Liveright forthcoming).

Notes

1. J. Ober, *Democracy and Knowledge*, Princeton University Press 2008.

2. W.E.B. DuBois, *Souls of Black Folk* [1903], in *W.E.B. DuBois: Writings*, Library of America 1987, p1.

Soundings

3. M.E. Warren, *Democracy and Association*, Princeton University Press 2000.

4. See Glenn C. Loury, *The Anatomy of Racial Inequality*, Harvard University Press 2002; and 'A Dynamic Theory of Racial Income Differences', in Phyllis Wallace and Annette LaMond (eds), *Women, Minorities and Employment Discrimination*, Lexington Books 1977; also E. Anderson, *The Imperative of Integration*, Princeton University Press 2010; and R. Rothstein, 'Racial Segregation and Black Student Achievement', in Allen and Reich (eds), *Education, Justice, and Democracy*, Chicago University Press 2013.

5. Samuel Bowles, Glenn C. Loury and Rajiv Sethi, 'Group inequality', in *Journal of the European Economic Association*, forthcoming: www.columbia.edu/~rs328/GroupInequality.pdf.

6. A. Lareau, *Unequal Childhoods: Class, Race, and Family Life*, 2nd ed, University of California Press 2011.

7. Ober, *Democracy and Knowledge*; S. Szreter, and M. Woolcock, 'Health by association? Social capital, social theory, and the political economy of public health', *Int. J. Epidemiol* 33 (4), 2004.

8. See P. Bourdieu, 'The forms of capital', in J. Richardson (ed), *Handbook of Theory and Research for the Sociology of Education*, Greenwood Press, 1986; J. Coleman, 'Social capital in the creation of human capital', *American Journal of Sociology* 1988; Robert Putnam, *Making Democracy Work: Civic Traditions in Modern Italy*, Princeton University Press 1993.

9. Marc S. Granovetter, 'The Strength of Weak Ties', *American Journal of Sociology* 78 1978; Szreter & Woolcock, 'Health by association?'.

10. Granovetter, *The Strength of Weak Ties*.

11. For the effects of connectedness on education, see Matthew Jackson, 'Social Structure, Segregation, and Economic Behavior', Nancy Schwartz Memorial Lecture in April 2007, revised 5.2.09: http://papers.ssrn.com/abstract=1530885; Lareau, *Unequal Childhoods*; J. Ludwig, H. F. Ladd & G. J. Duncan, 'Urban Poverty and Educational Outcomes', *Brookings-Wharton Papers on Urban Affairs* 2001; for social mobility and knowledge transmission see Granovetter, 'The Strength of Weak Ties'; Jackson, 'Social Structure …'; for creativity see Page 2011.

12. See Rajiv Sethi and Muhamet Yildiz, 'Public Disagreement', in *American*

A connected society

Economic Journal: Microeconomics, 4(3) 2012; Ober, *Democracy and Knowledge*; and John Dewey [1927] (ed. Melvin Rogers), *The Public and Its Problems*, Penn State 2012.

13. See D.S. Allen, *Talking to Strangers*, University of Chicago Press 2004; and J. Sidanius, S. Levin, C. van Laar and D.O. Sears, *The Diversity Challenge: Social Identity and Intergroup Relations on the College Campus*, Russell Sage Foundation 2008.

14. P.M. Bromberg, *The Shadow of the Tsunami: the Growth of the Relational Mind*, Routledge 2011; A. Honneth, 'Integrity and Disrespect: Principles of a Conception of Morality Based on a Theory of Recognition', *Political Theory* 20(2) 1992.

15. Allen, *Talking to Strangers*.

16 S. Moglen, 'Sharing Knowledge, Practicing Democracy: A Vision for the Twenty-First-Century University', in Allen and Reich, op cit.

REVIEWS

Can Labour break away from centralism?

Neal Lawson

Jon Wilson, *Letting Go: How Labour can learn to stop worrying and trust the people,* Fabian Society 2012

The British labour movement has been running on thin air for longer than it cares to recognise: in some respects New Labour could be seen as a valiant attempt to breathe life into it - but it turned out to be a case of go-faster stripes rather than a fundamental overhaul. What the much needed and essential transformation could look like is brilliantly covered by Jon Wilson in this short tract from, of all places, the Fabian Society. Well done to them for publishing it.

Labourism is based on a deal that goes something like this: you elect us (the Labour Party) and we will do socialism for you and to you; the people will be passive and grateful recipients of Labour's magnificence. The deal is encapsulated in many aspects of Labour's words and actions, but perhaps the best example was when Gordon Brown and Ed Balls went round telling anyone who would listen that they had lifted x million children out of poverty. You could almost feel their muscles ripple as they took on this historic, worthy and personal task. And of course in some ways they did accomplish something. They concocted a system of smoke and mirrors that managed for a while to give people living in poverty a bit more money. But it could never last. It was delivered through a giant redistributive Ponzi scheme that was too clever by half - one that took by stealth and gave by stealth. But it wasn't political action, it was technical device. And with no attempt to establish

Reviews

a moral public basis for redistribution the system had no chance of survival in the long term - and it has now gone the same way as neo-endogenous growth theory.

The Labourism deal is also summed up in the phrase 'our people', used by many Labour politicians when talking about the people who vote for them. The people, it would seem, belong to Labour. And this deal is entrenched in the 1945 moment - that now almost mythical time when a specific conjuncture of class, war and technology created the conditions for a top-down and centre-out version of socialism.

Labour tries to recreate that moment again and again: elect enough of the right Labour politicians to control the state and they will make socialism happen. There can't be anything wrong with the strategy - it worked once in 1945 and so it can and must work again.

But if there is one feature, above all, which manifests itself in our current public and economic lives, it is the shift from 'them to us' - the shift from a way of being (for both organisations and individuals) that is centralised and hierarchical to a world that is decentralised and horizontal. And the implications of this are profound.

We are currently witnessing the breaking up of the old tectonic plates. The ongoing crisis at the BBC - an archetypal ancient centralised institution - is evidence of the cumbersome and ineffectual nature of this type of antiquated structure. But all our big old institutions are in crisis. The media in general, banking, the police and the political establishment - all are finding themselves unable to cope, react or adjust to new pressures and demands. Old systems that are closed, rigid, hard and hierarchical are finding it increasingly tough when dealing with new systems that are open, malleable, soft and horizontal.

The process of change and adaptation will not be easy or simple. Paradigm shifts are always a slow and messy burn. And what is happening cannot be thought about in terms of a pendulum swing between right and left. There is no natural political winner from the 'them to us' switch. The new devolved and decentralised forms can be privatised and individualised as much as they can be 'publicised' and socialised. Much of this new 'us' world is built around technology, the morality of which is strictly neutral. It can end up with Amazon or Avaaz.

The switch gives progressives an opening, but only if we can tear ourselves away from the essentially Leninist/Fordist model that says 'socialism is what a Labour government does'. The rusted levers of the central state cannot cope with the complexity of the dispersed systems of the new world. People want to do things for themselves, and where and when they can't things will go wrong. As my good friend Jeremy Gilbert says, 'You cannot outsource socialism or the socialisation of your children to the market or the state - you have to co-produce it by getting involved and investing part of yourself in it. It's the only way things really work'.

More than anything else, the democratisation of our common life must be the motif that runs through the radical politics of the future. In economic development the emphasis should be on local democratic ownership; and the same vision should be applied to comprehensive schooling and health; while public services such as the railways could be taken back into public ownership, but in new and more democratic forms.

The contours of the new world can be seen all around us - in peer-to peer design, production and servicing, in online banks like Zopa, where people lend to each other and cut out the old banks, and in Wikipedia, our first port of call on any research project; it can be seen both in political campaigning vehicles like 38 Degrees (in which over one million decide the issue of the day and then make the campaign happen) and on-the-ground change through organisations like Locality.

The struggle of the future will be to find ways of knitting together a social and economic fabric that enables us to be creative and innovative the best way we can - with others. The future will be negotiated, with alliances formed and reformed around different issues; and the thread that runs through it all won't be a single party, but a belief in the capacity of people collectively to shape their world.

Jon Wilson here succinctly tells the story of why and how Labour should start changing course and trusting the people. He outlines a series of measures that point to the direction of change that is needed; for example, a shift from guidelines and targets to guarantees; the creation of stakeholders' boards; and the election of institutional leaders by assemblies. In addition, this new trusting politics would require new institutions, such as the Parents Union that has done much in the USA to improve school standards.

But I fear it will be more of a task than Jon lets on. So deeply entrenched is the myth of 1945 and the deal of votes-for-delivery that the movement might not be capable of making the shift to this new world. The idea of self-management simply has no traction within the Labour Party or the unions. It either doesn't fit as part of

Reviews

the deal, or is viewed as class compromise. Production is left to the bosses: all the workers need do is seek to secure as many crumbs from the table as possible.

New Labour extended this elite form of socialism rather than challenging it. As the forces of the labour movement weakened, the leadership felt compelled to tighten its grip on the party, the state and the country. This distrust of everyone, including the party membership, combined with the forces of global competition and the need to manage a 24-news cycle, meant that the control-freak tendency - not the democratic tendency - took on an ever-firmer grip.

Jon Wilson beautifully tells us the spell must be broken. But can it? Let's see.

An exercise in self justification

Ken Spours

Andrew Adonis, *Education, Education, Education: Reforming England's Schools*, Biteback Publishing 2012

This is a book with serious consequences, not least because Andrew Adonis thinks he will be making Labour policy for 2015; a view shared by sections of the right-wing media. Even if Adonis doesn't quite exercise the political influence he and others think he has, this book still requires scrutiny because it mixes myth and truth, and it has gained some traction in the political middle ground between the extremities of Michael Gove's neo-conservative revolution and the education arguments of the left.

It is important from the outset to understand its overarching narrative. As others have commented, this is a book largely dedicated to justifying Adonis's academies strategy. Adonis argues that comprehensive schools failed, mainly because of the deficiencies of local authorities and the education profession, and a new start was therefore needed to save 'comprehensives'. This was achieved by creating schools independent of local authorities, supported by private sponsorship funds and strong leadership. He goes on to suggest that Labour needs more of the same next time round, and that the private school sector should step in to rescue maintained education. He also ventures into the area of curriculum and qualifications by supporting a divided baccalaureate system of IB-type A-levels and a separate Technical Baccalaureate for those not suited to the academic track. It is a narrative that proposes neoliberal means to achieve social democratic ends.

Its assertions about academies in particular have been taken to task by a number of reviewers, notably Melissa Benn, Richard Pring and the Socialist Education

Reviews

Association.[1] They point to his lack of faith in the 'public' and a belief in the power of the private, privileged and powerful to rescue the concept of the comprehensive. They note his avoidance of international evidence that suggests that the highest performing national systems, such as that of Finland, have relatively no private sector to speak of and little education division. They argue that the logic of his reforms leads to national centralisation rather than to real school freedoms; that his assertions about the miraculous performance of academies do not hold water; and that non-academy schools have made significant progress in recent years.

In this regard, the book revolves around two related exaggerations. The first is its apocalyptic view of state education at the end of the Conservative era - with the blame being laid at the door of comprehensive schools rather than Thatcherism. The second is the greatly exaggerated contribution it attributes to academies in raising educational standards under New Labour; whereas, particularly in London, improved standards can most plausibly be seen to be the result of a combination of policies, including investment in infrastructure, a focus on leadership and school improvement, London Challenge and Teach First. Rather than acknowledging the effects of all of these on the system as a whole, Adonis chooses to devote most of his book to a pet project, and one that started with the exceptional rather than the general - the story of the transformation of Hackney Downs to the Mossbourne Academy.

But the real issue at the centre of this book is not a squabble about New Labour's academies programme and its effects on performance, but its political implications for what is happening now under Michael Gove and the Conservatives. Kenneth Baker, writing in the *Daily Telegraph*, called *Education, Education, Education* a 'remarkable book', which should be compulsory reading for the Cameron cabinet. He went on to state that Gove is essentially building on the Adonis foundation, which is one that any future government would find to be irreversible. Adonis has in fact had little to say about the ways in which his policies have paved the way for the Conservative privatising revolution, other than declaring his support for free schools and for institutionally determined teacher pay. The right knows a friend when they see one.

The book starts and finishes around the theme of a 'future yet unmade', but what kind of future? Adonis writes as if a revolutionising Conservative government does not exist and that Labour, if it wins in 2015, can take up where it left off. By the next election, however, the English education landscape will comprise a mosaic of fragmented institutions being run by private academy chains regulated from Whitehall. It will be one of the most centralised and politicised education systems in the western world - and one in which communities are denied a voice.

Labour, possibly working with other political parties, will therefore have to find ways of bringing all types of education institutions together at the local level to collaborate for the benefit of all. It will need to create new means of reinvigorating local democracy and new forms of engagement between local political representatives and schools - for example through locally elected and representative local education boards. But on these crucial issues, *Education, Education, Education* remains silent: Adonis appears not to have sufficient belief in local democracy, popular participation and the principle of collaboration.

Amidst the silences and the gaps in this book lies a responsibility for the left. It has to work in an open and alliance-based way to develop a vibrant vision of education - public rather than private, democratic rather than centralist, unified rather than divided, and with an expansive and outward-looking professionalism. This book is important, not as a result of its compelling vision of education, but because it is a wake-up call to those who seek to prevent Labour from sleepwalking into an education policy that barely comprehends what is happening before our eyes.

Notes

1. See Melissa Benn, 'Education, Education, Education', *Guardian*, 2.11.12; Richard Pring, 'Facts get in the way of academy success story', Letter, *Guardian*, 16.9.12; John Bolt, 'Andrew Adonis and his friends', at http://educevery.wordpress.com/2012/09/13/andrew-adonis-and-his-friends/.

A belated howl of grief

Ed Wallis

Peter Hook, *Unknown Pleasures. Inside Joy Division*, Simon & Schuster 2012

Joy Division were shocked into life by an electrical charge that coursed through mid-1970s culture: punk. When the Sex Pistols played at Manchester Free Trade Hall in 1976, the show was famously attended by only fifty people, yet spawned as many bands. Peter Hook, bass player and founder member of Joy Division and New Order, was there with his future band mate and sparring partner Bernard Sumner, as were Morrissey, Mark E Smith and - less often noted, to be fair - Mick Hucknall.

Music in the 1970s was detached from the energetic youth culture that spawned rock and roll in the 1950s; it had become the more rarefied preserve of the technically accomplished and expensively educated, mostly in the form of progressive rock. The arrival of punk said goodbye to all that: how thrilling for a 'working class tosser from Salford' - as Hook describes himself in *Unknown Pleasures* - to realise you didn't really need to be able to play to be in a band. The Sex Pistols seemed 'human' to Hook compared to other bands, which seemed 'so out of my league they might as well have lived on another planet'- 'the Sex Pistols, though: they looked like working-class tossers too'. This sensibility led not only to the formation of Warsaw, later Joy Division, but also to one of their defining features as a band: Hook's instantly recognisable melodic bass style came about by accident, a lack of technical proficiency meaning he only learned to play with three fingers, while a cheap amp forced him to play high up the fret board to make himself heard.

Hook's is a story wrapped in the northern, working-class culture he grew up with. He dwells on the minutiae of the class differences between him and his band mates: Sumner's family 'didn't exactly have pots of money but anything he wanted,

Soundings

he got'; Steve Morris's parents' house 'had *two* inside toilets, as well as central heating'. And settling scores with former colleagues holds the whip hand in the book's early pages - thus, whilst Hook makes more than clear his musical respect for Sumner, his presence in the book is prim, prissy and uptight. Hook's gripes recur: Sumner's unravelling of a sleeping bag after an early gig in Newcastle while his colleagues froze in the van - an act of foresight so alien to Hook it can only be processed as treachery; or his habit of disappearing when a fight broke out at a show (regular occurrences that Hook was in the thick of). 'Whoever it was who said that "no man is an island" never met Bernard', he writes. In fact the defensive tone that pervades much of *Unknown Pleasures* should probably be seen in the context of the broader and longstanding conflict between the two men.

Hook's style is more garrulous raconteur than author, and draws heavily on his 'gobby Manc' persona, but he is not unpleasant company as he rattles through his early years, and he poignantly captures 'wonderful, dirty old Salford': 'When I saw [the film] *Control* all those years later, I didn't even notice it was in black and white because it was exactly what my childhood had looked and felt like: dark and smoggy and brown, the colour of a wet cardboard box'.

The band traded on the chilly, grey aesthetic of their hometown until they were frozen in their prime, following the suicide of Ian Curtis in 1980. They left behind two near-perfect albums and thus became a group for whom the familiar tropes of so much music criticism are accurate descriptors rather than limp clichés: seminal, iconic, tragic. Two recent films - Anton Corbijn's austere *Control* and Michael Winterbottom's *24 Hour Party People* - attest to their story's potency. But it's a heavy legacy, and guilt lingers on every page as the story arcs inevitably to Curtis's death. Hook's amiably unreconstructed blokeishness takes on a more sinister aspect as the culture he celebrates becomes complicit in the book's central tragedy. He painfully describes the increasing frequency and violence of Curtis's epileptic seizures, including a particularly bad incident where Curtis knocked himself out on a sink when fitting. Commenting on this he writes: 'Guess what? We brought him round, he said he was alright and we carried on. I should call the book that, shouldn't I? *He Said He was All Right So We Carried On*'.

Hook was unaware of the scale of Curtis's problems at the time, and the book has clearly been a journey of discovery, aided not only by the 20-20 of hindsight but by twenty-first century perspectives on family life and mental illness. 'It's only recently

Reviews

that I've started to get a clear picture of the kind of shit Ian was going through and the very short timescale involved.' After 'working him to death', the band finally cancelled some gigs, but by then the jig was up. Perhaps today a manager, doctor or friend might be expected to intervene in such a situation - or might relieve some of the burden, attempt to instigate some semblance of 'work-life balance', find better care. Certainly the world Hook depicts is one where men didn't talk to each other about anything they were feeling or experiencing, no matter how severe or urgent. But as he reads today about the latest breakdown of a teen pop sensation or movie starlet, Hook perhaps may realise that the past isn't such a foreign country after all.

Ultimately, though, all he's left with is the guilt - 'that, like everybody else, I went along with Ian when he said he was alright; that I was so wrapped up in my own bit of me, of the band, that I never took the time to listen to his lyrics or him and think, *He really needs help.*' In amongst the bravado and bitterness, the fondness and fandom, *Unknown Pleasures* is a simple search for absolution - and a belated howl of grief for a friend.

Multiculturalism reloaded?

Mike Waite

Ted Cantle, *Interculturalism: the new era of cohesion and diversity*, Palgrave Macmillan 2012

Ted Cantle's achievement was to shape national policy on race relations during the years of New Labour government. He developed and applied the concept of 'community cohesion' through his overview report on the causes of the riots and disturbances in particular northern towns back in 2001; but the approaches which flowed from his analysis were quickly accepted as having widespread relevance. Councils across the country developed 'cohesion' work, using government grants to run specific projects, and 'mainstreaming' the approach into their general practice.

Why did this policy framework become established so rapidly? Firstly, it was based on concrete analysis of significant trends and problems. Cantle identified how different 'communities' live 'parallel lives'. He was alert to how social suspicions and distances had developed, but had not been acknowledged or addressed. Secondly, Cantle addressed a wider debate on 'multiculturalism'. In place since the late 1960s - though never uncontested - this policy framework was under severe pressure by the beginning of the twenty-first century, because of a series of connected social trends that served to undermine its coherence and credibility.

These developments included entrenched patterns of residential segregation in some areas; destabilising 'churn' in others; anxiety and resentment over resource allocation and access to provision such as housing and education; greater than anticipated migration from the formerly communist countries of the European

Reviews

Union, and the significant impact this had on local tax-funded services; and the way growing economic pressures opened up political space for sectional, identity-based and nationalist movements, including those drawing on persistent popular opposition to 'Europe'. Some argued that multiculturalism's recognition of racial and cultural communities, and its support for diverse lifestyles, had encouraged division and led to social fragmentation. The superficial celebration of 'steel bands and samosas' had been liberal blindness to real problems. Other 'opponents' of multiculturalism, ironically, chose this moment to assert a multiculturalist claim. Mixing playfulness, bullish confidence and subaltern pleading, nationalist politicians argued that 'all they wanted' was for the same rights to be afforded to 'the indigenous majority' as 'others' now enjoyed. Amongst all this, 'cohesion' stood against fragmentation. Whilst 'celebrating' difference, it supported projects to bolster what 'we all have in common' in a community, a city, a country.

Nobody ever said that achieving settlements between diversity and commonality would be easy, especially around contested issues and real disputes, including over the appropriate allowances that people should be afforded around identity-based 'needs' and 'rights'. And so the third strength of the cohesion agenda was flexibility: the way it could 'triangulate', and achieve policy 'balances' on successive concerns - including the far right's emergence; the questions raised by the July 2005 London transport bombings; and many local issues that generated identity based claims for 'fairness'.

As this suggests, 'cohesion' mapped out a field within which matters were handled, rather than providing prescriptive answers. And the field proved unstable. Campaigners for racial equality saw their agenda being undermined: surely their calls for 'positive action' and 'complaints' about discrimination pulled against the new emphasis on what 'we' all had in common? And after 7/7, some saw the Home Office's 'Prevent' strategy as 'targeting' Muslim youth. What government presented as a positive initiative was taken as adding to problems of stereotyping and panic, thereby alienating those 'reasonable' community members on whose support the programme's success depended.

Unstable policies need pushing in one direction or another, and the Coalition's approach, with far less project money available, has been to name 'integration' as the desirable social goal. This will tend to reproduce rather than resolves the instabilities in the policy field.

Soundings

However, though the idea of 'integration' sometimes provokes knee-jerk opposition from left-wingers and liberals, it is clear that the government are not proposing integration in any sense of suppressing multiplicity and diversity on the terms of those who are dominant. Whilst not allowing free rein to multiplicity, 'integration' can be an interactive project to bring together and give order to multiplicity, through processes of negotiation, agreement and relationship building. In this context, it is to Cantle's credit that he has neither simply moved with the policy field, nor settled for reasserting 'the cohesion agenda'. His thinking through of the limits and tensions in the earlier policy he developed has generated a stimulating book.

The 'interculturalism' he proposes, however, is unlikely to have the practical impact that 'community cohesion' did. In spite of the examples and facts the book marshals, key themes are theoretical and abstract. The lack of clarity in Cantle's main argument has led to a debate over whether his 'interculturalism' really amounts to anything more than a call for the type of interaction and mutuality with diversity that would make multiculturalism effective.

Cantle, however, is adamant that he's proposing a new approach. He argues that it is needed because 'multiculturalism has failed'. This insistent tone is most marked when he is setting the context within which the new framework is needed: 'we cannot stop the process of globalisation: the world is more interconnected than ever before'. Cantle believes that the impact of globalisation is creating more inward-looking and fractured communities, as people 'cling to more traditional identities and "hunker down"', and that this has been exacerbated by some political leaders, 'who have seized the opportunity to pursue singular and populist campaigns, which reinforce divisions'. He argues that instead we should 'adjust' to the 'era of super diversity and globalisation'.

The book's vision of a unified world, in which all manner of local difficulties have been resolved, is essentially utopian. This is a positive vision, and of course is preferable to the politics of demoralisation and hatred which often shape particularistic, identity-based politics. On the book's cover, Yasmin Alibhai-Brown goes so far as to suggest that Cantle's proposed 'conceptual shift' is so compelling that it could 'pull the world back from dystopia'.

Unfortunately, Cantle's interculturalism is also utopian in the sense of being a pitch to the good sense of enlightened people. It sets out an ideal system or

Reviews

settlement, rather than charting a way forward from current social trends and political opportunities.

And, like all policy visions presented in universal terms, it actually itself reflects a particular outlook. Cantle suggests that 'cosmopolitanism' is 'underway through the everyday processes of international travel and communication, the integration of business, the development of transnational education markets, the social and cultural intermixing and the consequent emergence of multi-layered affinities and identities'. The resulting task is to create 'a more global conception of ourselves' through developing 'cultural navigation skills and intercultural competence'. But whose 'universal' outlook is this? It is a long way from many people's experience. Many feel current trends as disconnection, isolation and the closing down of opportunities. Understandably, some people respond by shaping and fastening onto ready and local identities. Practical politics needs to relate to these in ways which involve 'taking sides' on key issues. Building consensus on these is not easy.

Ed Miliband's December 2012 speech on integration highlighted such difficulties. He proposed that all publicly funded workers should speak good English if they interacted with residents and service users. He argued that newcomers to Britain and foreign-born schoolchildren should learn English, and that this drive should be promoted over the practice of translating into other languages. For some, this was 'dog whistle' politics: not so coded signals to racists that Labour, too, is impatient with immigrants. For others, Miliband did not go far enough in addressing the serious challenge of how to achieve integration at a time of great demographic change.

Building better race relations will mean working through difficult issues and real differences of opinion. And increasing people's confidence in dealing with these matters will be a big part of this process. In his book, Cantle does highlight some useful approaches, such as mediation and dialogue between people with different identities and points of view. But these are most likely to be successful if they start from people's lived experience in neighbourhoods, businesses and agencies, rather than being based on a view that 'globalisation' is a force of nature to which resistance is futile.

Neal Lawson is the Chair of Compass and author of *All Consuming* (Penguin

2009). **Ken Spours** is Professor of Education at the Institute of Education, University of London, and Convenor of Compass Education Group. **Ed Wallis** is is Head of Editorial at the Fabian Society. **Mike Waite** works for Burnley Council, where his responsibilities have included managing community cohesion programmes. His paper *Combining Diversity with Common Citizenship* was published by the Joseph Rowntree Charitable Trust in 2009. He writes here in a personal capacity.

Has multiculturalism in Britain retreated?

Varun Uberoi and Tariq Modood

If properly understood, multiculturalism continues to flourish in Britain.

Scholars who are critical and supportive of multiculturalism note how it is in 'retreat' or in question in different countries as leading politicians are rejecting it.[1] Britain is often cited as a place in which this retreat or questioning occurs.[2] Certainly British politicians and commentators criticise multiculturalism, but it is often unclear what precisely is being criticised.[3] Even when critics say that what they are discussing is 'state multiculturalism', nothing is said about what this is, or how it differs from 'multiculturalism', and neither is self-explanatory.[4] We therefore begin by specifying three inter-related ways in which multiculturalism can be understood, before going on to show why it is questionable to claim that leading British politicians are distancing themselves from any of them. We then identify the superficial nature of what it is that these leading politicians are actually rejecting, and the benefit, even for critics, of adopting our understandings of multiculturalism.

Understandings of multiculturalism

Like equality, justice, fairness and class, multiculturalism can be conceived of in different ways, but we focus on three inter-related understandings of it.[5] First, multiculturalism is often said to denote a culturally diverse citizenry, or what may be called a 'multicultural society'. The latter seems inescapable as cultural diversity is in-eliminable 'without an unacceptable level of coercion', and perhaps not even

Soundings

then as regional or class based cultural differences would remain even if those based on immigration were removed.[6] But a state can react to a culturally diverse citizenry in different ways. It could *try* to remain neutral between cultural groups and not favour any of them. But this is difficult, as the language, norms and sensibilities used to regulate the collective affairs of its citizens have to come from somewhere and are usually the cultural traits of at least one group. Instead a state could try to assimilate cultural minorities by aiming to make them as indistinguishable from the cultural majority as possible. If assimilation is voluntary, or as a state aim it is restricted to obviously morally repugnant practices, it is usually uncontroversial. But if it goes further it infringes individual freedom, and creates or reinforces a hierarchy among citizens by encouraging some to conform to others even though each is meant to be equal. For such reasons, Canada, Britain and Australia abandoned policies of assimilation in the 1960s; formal and informal *policies* of multiculturalism then followed; and thus a second way to understand multiculturalism emerged.[7]

A *policy* of multiculturalism usually aims to reduce fear of cultural difference, as well as the inequality, exclusion and disadvantage that are often experienced by cultural minorities in subtle yet significant ways. For example, when the state uses the language, norms and sensibilities of the cultural majority in its political institutions, or establishes only their religion in them or teaches only their history in schools, cultural minorities are excluded and treated unequally, despite being citizens who are entitled to equal treatment. Similarly, if public services are offered *only* in the *lingua franca*, citizens who are less proficient with the language - like recent immigrants or older cultural minorities - are disadvantaged, as these services are more difficult for them to use than they are for other citizens. Multicultural education in schools and promoting race equality are thus used to reduce fear of cultural difference, while anti-discrimination laws, legal exemptions for minority religious practices, providing public services in different languages and other measures are used to reduce the inequality, exclusion and disadvantage that cultural minorities suffer. Different combinations of such measures have been called a policy of multiculturalism in different countries, but if fear of cultural difference reduces, along with the inequality, exclusion and disadvantage cultural minorities incur, the nation will change, and it is unclear what it will become or how to sustain a political commitment to such change. Multiculturalism in a third sense of what some call an 'ideology' thus emerges.[8] This ideology on close inspection is often a 'vision for the nation' that explains how the nation is changing and will continue to change, and

Has multiculturalism in Britain retreated?

helps to foster a commitment to the trajectory the nation is on.[9] Such a vision for the nation was offered by the Commission for Multi-Ethnic Britain; and different policies of multiculturalism in different countries have also offered similar visions.[10] Yet this 'vision for the nation' is the least well understood way of thinking about multiculturalism, partly because it is the most complex. So we will now spend some time explaining it.

Typically the entities we call nations have features like a homeland, language, history, traditions, symbols and legal and political institutions. Such features constitute a nation's identity because they collectively make it what it is; hence if asked what Britain, France or Germany are, our answers invoke such features, and if these features change we think the nation has too. But *members* of a nation are also often said to have common features and this does not necessarily mean that they are ethnically similar; in many nations, like Switzerland, Canada and India, they are not. Yet members of a nation often *have* common features in a different sense of believing that features of their nation - like its homeland, history, traditions and so on - are *theirs*. They do so because they have a sense of what their *nation's* identity is which we often call their *national* identities; and such identities are shared with others *not* as we share a cake by dividing it, but as two or more people share an opinion or a view.[11] Indeed, a nation's identity and people's sense of it are related, as changes to the former tend to destabilise the latter. Thus as Britain's imperial, military and economic might were disappearing, debates began to emerge not only about what Britain was becoming but also about what it meant to *be* British.[12]

In a vision for the nation, then, a nation has an identity and people have a sense of it, but both the former and the latter can be disturbed by globalisation, minority-nationalism, supra-national institutions and so on.[13] Multiculturalism in the first sense of the emergence of a culturally diverse citizenry is another such disturbance, as those with a sense of what the nation is note that their homeland is now also home to others, and that features of the nation, like its legal and political institutions, affect many citizens who do not see them as *theirs*. Thus features of the nation that once exclusively belonged to the majority are now shared, and the widespread affinity for them that could once be assumed can now no longer be; and so, understandably, people's sense of their nation's identity is disturbed. But if cultural minorities are citizens this disturbance is necessary, as they are more likely to be treated unequally if they are seen as outsiders and not as part of the

Soundings

nation. Similarly, as the cultural majority's language, norms and values are usually present in features of the nation all citizens are supposed to be equal in, like legal and political institutions, but those of cultural minorities are not, the latter are treated unequally. Short of abandoning a commitment to equal treatment and citizenship, multiculturalism in our first sense helps to force a re-examination of the features that comprise a nation's identity and people's sense of it; but it also makes both of these more important. After all, a culturally diverse citizenry is also more susceptible to division, competition and conflict between cultural groups. A nation's identity is thus important, as people's sense of it will convey to them that, despite their differences, they share a homeland, history, language, traditions, institutions, symbols and other features that make them, *inter alia*, a group. This helps them to take collective action, accept collectively binding decisions and conceive a common good. Contrary then to what various critics claim, multiculturalists have long acknowledged the importance of a nation's identity and people's sense of it, but they also note how both can come to include cultural minorities as they do change.

Hence Britain's identity today differs from what it was a century ago, as do people's British identities, and the measures within a policy of multiculturalism that are described above help over time to make such changes. Anti-discrimination measures and legal exemptions for minority religious practices help to make features of the nation like legal and political institutions more inclusive, as does these institutions promoting race equality and delivering public services in different languages. As features of the nation become more inclusive, so, by definition, does its identity. But these more inclusive legal and political institutions over time also help shape people's sense of what the nation is, as does multicultural education in schools, which shows children why different groups comprise the nation, shape its history and nature, and call it 'home'. Some may resist this education, but if it is taught throughout their school lives and to successive generations, some may not. Policies of multiculturalism are thus a means to *help* make a nation's identity and people's sense of it more inclusive over time - but not wholly different. If features of the nation that the cultural majority believe to be theirs were to change completely, the sense of loss that follows could prevent an affinity for what the nation has become, and could cause a backlash against minorities. But it is also impossible for a nation's identity and people's sense of it to become wholly different, as both remain strongly conditioned by their starting points of the existing nation's identity and people's existing senses of

Has multiculturalism in Britain retreated?

it - both of which, as noted above, the cultural majority are usually favoured in. Hence the Swann Report said:

> we are not seeking to fit ethnic minorities into a mould which was originally cast for a society, relatively homogenous ... nor to break this mould completely and replace it with one which is in all senses foreign ... We are instead looking to recast the mould into a form which retains the fundamental principles of the original, but within a broader pluralist conspectus.[14]

What is envisaged, then, is more inclusive versions of the *existing* nation's identity, and people's *existing* sense of it - versions that are worthy of commitment as they include the cultural majority *and* cultural minorities.

This 'vision for the nation' thus explains that multiculturalism in our first sense is one of many factors that can disturb a nation's identity and people's sense of it, but this is necessary and it also makes both more important; while multiculturalism in our second sense of a policy helps to make both more inclusive though not unrecognisable. These three understandings of multiculturalism are thus interrelated as they help one another to emerge, and each relates to a nation's identity and people's sense of it. But is it plausible to claim that leading British politicians are rejecting multiculturalism in any of these senses?

Where's the retreat?

We accept that multiculturalism is criticised frequently by leading politicians.[15] But few of them claim that a culturally diverse citizenry is problematic, and many of them explicitly endorse the latter.[16] Indeed, when even groups like the English Defence League make gestures towards welcoming a culturally diverse citizenry, it shows just how hard it is to disagree *publicly* with this understanding of multiculturalism.[17] But David Cameron criticised 'state multiculturalism' in 2011, and this suggests that it may be the policy that is unpopular. Certainly scholars who identify a 'retreat' in Britain focus on such a policy. But the most prominent scholar to do so has resiled from this position; and this is not surprising as it is difficult to identify the multiculturalist measures and budgets that have been cut.[18]

Legal exemptions for minority religious practices remain, as do anti-discrimination measures. The aims of multicultural education remain in the English education curriculum.[19] It is unclear whether or not race equality is promoted less than it once was, or whether public services are no longer delivered in different languages. Certainly the latter has been criticised. But there is no country-wide evidence to suggest that these two measures are less prevalent than before; and even if it is the case that some local authorities are no longer offering public services in different languages, the retreat of one measure among many does not logically indicate the retreat of an entire policy, especially since other measures - like anti-discrimination laws and minority faith schools - have actually increased since 2001.[20]

But supporters and critics of multiculturalism have suggested that it has retreated as a policy since the 2001 riots and 9/11 because the priority has been fostering 'community cohesion'.[21] However, compared to cutting measures and budgets, fostering community cohesion is at best an inexact indicator of any retreat, and for it to be a plausible indicator at all it must conflict with a policy of multiculturalism and it is unclear why it does.[22] This is partly because community cohesion is a notoriously vague idea that those suggesting such a conflict fail to clarify - and we too cannot here systematically explore what it denotes.[23] But as community members are not literally stuck together, 'community cohesion' is a metaphor that would appear to describe what the report introducing the term called 'helping micro-communities to gel or mesh into an integrated whole'.[24] The reference to 'micro-communities' suggests that this 'gelling' or 'meshing' focuses on a local level, but the 'integrated whole' can also be national. Hence the report also said while there could be no return to 'a dominant or mono-culturalist view of nationality', there must be agreement on 'some common elements of nationhood' (pp18-19). The aim here appears to be for different communities to possess some commonalities and feel like a united group; and as a policy of multiculturalism helps to make, as we have seen, nationhood more inclusive, so that more can be part of this group, it is difficult to see a conflict. But some might argue that a policy of multiculturalism prevents local communities from feeling like a group by dividing them residentially. However, it seems a strange claim that measures like anti-discrimination legislation, legal exemptions for minority religious practices and so on foster residential separation, especially as research suggests that poverty, higher birth rates among some groups and higher mortality rates among others are the drivers.[25] In short, fostering community cohesion cannot easily be used even as an inexact indicator of a

Has multiculturalism in Britain retreated?

retreating policy of multiculturalism, for the simple reason that it is unclear why the two necessarily conflict.

But perhaps leading politicians are now less inclined to advocate multiculturalism when it takes the form of a 'vision for the nation'? Certainly there are many such visions, but recall that in this one it is crucial that a nation's identity and people's sense of it become more inclusive. A pertinent indicator, then, would be examining whether leading politicians are less inclined to advocate making Britain's identity, people's British identities, or what for brevity can be called 'Britishness', more inclusive.[26] Multiculturalists first talked about this goal in 1974;[27] and the 1985 Swann Report into the education of ethnic minority children also emphasised this goal, as did other leading multiculturalists after the Rushdie Affair.[28] Doing so has *seemingly* influenced liberal nationalists like David Miller, who by the 1990s came to advocate making Britishness more inclusive.[29] But this goal seemed unpopular among leading politicians as late as 2000; when the Commission for Multi-Ethnic Britain argued in their report, amongst other things, that '*political leaders* should ... lead the country in re-imagining Britain ... and in ensuring the national story is inclusive', it was attacked in the media.[30] Home Secretary Jack Straw said he disagreed with part of the report partly because in his view Britishness had already become more inclusive.[31] At this time William Hague was also suggesting in speeches that Britishness had already become more inclusive, and, like leading Labour figures, did not mention aiding this process.[32] Making 'Britishness' more inclusive was seemingly not something leading politicians would advocate even in 2000 - but they do now.

Thus the last Labour government led a debate about Britishness, and introduced measures aimed at those whose British identities are most malleable i.e. children and immigrants who want to become citizens. During citizenship ceremonies new citizens now pledge allegiance to the political features of Britain which were also equated with being British in a pamphlet that many of them were assessed on.[33] Children now also learn about 'the changing nature of UK society, including the diversity of ideas, beliefs, cultures, identities, traditions, perspectives and values that are shared'.[34] By equating Britishness with Britain's political features and its diversity, the Labour government were promoting what we have called elsewhere a civic multicultural national identity.[35] Civic nationhood seems inclusive because the political features defining the nation can be shared regardless of ethnicity; but there was also the multicultural component where Britain is defined not just by its multi-ethnic mix but also by the way it has historically accommodated difference and is doing so today. Indeed John Denham noted: 'While a modern British identity will … draw heavily on the history of the White British majority, we cannot discover Britishness in that history alone; it will have to draw on the histories of all those who now make up our country'.[36] Such claims are not restricted to Labour politicians as similar ones are now being made by Education Secretary, Michael Gove, who has discussed Britishness in civic terms, but also in 2009 said 'Britishness is about a mongrel identity'.[37] There is, again, then, a multicultural component to this Britishness; in opposition Pauline Neville Jones, a figure regarded as being on the right of the Conservative Party, led a review group which argued: 'we need to rebuild Britishness in ways which … allow us to understand the contributions which all traditions, whether primarily ethnic or national, have made and are making to our collective identity'.[38] And in his 2011 Munich speech, Cameron criticised 'state multiculturalism', but also advocated 'a … national identity that is *open to everyone*'.[39] Where Thatcher and Major discussed preserving traditional forms of Britishness, their successors emphasise the inclusivity of its civic and multicultural components, and, like leading Labour figures, seem more keen to make Britishness more inclusive than their predecessors even in 2000. So not only is it difficult to plausibly argue that multiculturalism has retreated if it is understood as referring to a culturally diverse citizenry or to a policy; it has also seemingly advanced when understood as a vision for the nation.[40]

Conclusion

It seems implausible, then, that leading politicians are distancing themselves from these three inter-related understandings of multiculturalism. But what if the retreat is from a different understanding of multiculturalism that denotes promoting separation and division?[41] This understanding reflects a broader climate of opinion in which commentators and even some scholars claim that multiculturalism is divisive, and can sometimes add that it also *forces* people into separate groups.[42] Yet it is unclear who or what is promoting this separation and division as no evidence of multiculturalist ideas or measures that do so are offered. Certainly multiculturalists focus on groups, but this is *not* because members of such groups share all the same traits; rather it is because they share a range of different ones

Has multiculturalism in Britain retreated?

such that they can be conceived as or they *self*-identify as, *inter alia*, a group. This is different from forcing or inadvertently coercing group membership or indeed from proving that multiculturalist measures do either.[43] Further, multiculturalists have long rejected separation and division; hence they identify how unity and belonging can be fostered among *all* citizens.[44] Finally, policies of multiculturalism in different countries have been used to promote such unity;[45] and have not inadvertently caused phenomena like residential separation in the UK, because, as noted above, there are other drivers for such separation.[46] This understanding of multiculturalism as promoting division thus seems unrelated to what multiculturalists claim, what policies of multiculturalism aim for, and the available evidence of their impact. It is, then, a caricature, but it functions like a stereotype as it is intuitively appealing and thus widely believed, but is also pejorative and an inaccurate depiction of what it claims to relate to. And the more leading politicians and others assert this understanding, the more they help to normalise the climate of opinion it reflects and shapes. But this understanding cannot be asserted *plausibly* without explaining why its inaccuracy is irrelevant. And if this is what leading British politicians are retreating from, then they are rejecting an inaccurate understanding of multiculturalism, while endorsing or remaining silent about more accurate understandings of it.

Of course, rejecting this caricature can be deliberate or not. Some, like Will Kymlicka, suspect international organisations like UNESCO are 'aware they are presenting a caricature', and argue that 'to preserve the commitment to diversity' they 'need to drop the poisoned term of multiculturalism …'.[47] But this in turn reveals another possibility: that it may just be the word 'multiculturalism' that leading politicians are objecting to. As one former MP recently said at an event we participated in, 'multiculturalism is a boo word'; politicians thus may be unsure what they mean by it, but they know politically they have to oppose it. But if leading politicians are rejecting an inaccurate understanding of multiculturalism, or indeed just the word itself, their complaint is superficial as it does not reach more accurate understandings of multiculturalism.

Such hostility may nonetheless corrode political support for the more accurate understandings. But this is not inevitable. After all, leading British politicians have exhibited hostility to multiculturalism since the 2001 riots and 9/11, but since then they have also passed multiculturalist measures such as the Incitement to Religious

Hatred Act and certain public duties attached to the Equalities Act.[48] Likewise, the Canadian policy of multiculturalism was criticised strongly even after the 1988 Multiculturalism Act was passed, and its measures were subject to large budgetary cuts in the 1990s.[49] But today it remains popular; the measures that comprise it were retained and are among the most advanced multiculturalist measures in the world. Similarly, the Australian policy of multiculturalism was exposed to the same kind of criticism in the 1990s, but the Gillard government has renewed its commitment to it.[50] Hostility to a caricature of multiculturalism may corrode political support for its more accurate understandings but the unofficial British policy and the official Canadian and Australian policies have been resilient and durable despite such hostility.

But beyond politicians, other prominent critics of multiculturalism would also seemingly not object to all of our understandings of multiculturalism. Some of them might agree that the rate of future immigration should be reduced.[51] But few of these prominent critics *now* reject a multicultural citizenry, as they recognise, as we say above, that it is inescapable without an unacceptable level of coercion, and, like leading politicians, they *now* also publicly advocate what multiculturalists began to in 1974, namely 'Britishness' being more inclusive.[52] Thus when such critics talk about ensuring '*everyone* can see something of themselves' in the nation,[53] they are unknowingly advocating an idea that originates with multiculturalists.[54] Yet even the most thought provoking of these critics assumes that a policy of multiculturalism is divisive despite the above evidence and arguments to the contrary; and it is thus multiculturalism as a policy that they seemingly object to.[55] We have seen, however, that such a policy helps to make a nation's identity and people's sense of it more inclusive; thus the understanding of multiculturalism such critics object to, when accurately understood, helps to achieve the inclusive nations that they themselves espouse. Even such prominent critics then can gain both from reconsidering the understanding of multiculturalism that they reject, and - along with leading politicians - considering what exactly it is they are objecting to.

Notes

1. For example R. Bauböck, 'Farewell to Multiculturalism?', *Journal of International Migration and Integration*, 3, 2002, p2; C. Joppke, 'The Retreat

Has multiculturalism in Britain retreated?

of Multiculturalism in the Liberal State: Theory and Policy', *British Journal of Sociology*, 55, 2004, p243; T. Modood, *Still Not Easy Being British*, Trentham Books 2010, p6.

2. Joppke, 'Retreat ...', p249; D. McGhee, *The End of Multiculturalism?*, Open University Press 2008, pp99-103.

3. G. Brown, 'We Need a United Kingdom', *Telegraph*, 13.1.07; D. Goodhart, 'Too Diverse', *Prospect*, February 2004.

4. D. Cameron, Speech, Munich Security Conference, 5.2.11.

5. Modood, *Still Not Easy* ..., pp6-7.

6. B. Parekh, *Rethinking Multiculturalism*, Macmillan, p196.

7. V. Uberoi, 'Do Policies of Multiculturalism Change National Identities?', *Political Quarterly*, 79, 2008.

8. D. Miller, 'Multiculturalism and the Welfare State: Theoretical Reflections', in K. Banting and W. Kymlicka (eds), *Multiculturalism and the Welfare State*, Oxford University Press, p326.

9. C. Taylor, 'Interculturalism or Multiculturalism', *Philosophy and Social Criticism*, 38, 2012.

10. Uberoi, 'Do Policies ...', p411; G.B. Levey, 'Multicultural Political Thought in Australian Perspective', in G. B. Levey (ed), *Political Theory and Australian Multiculturalism*, Berghahn Books 2008, pp6-7.

11. This idea occurred to us when reading a draft of Bhikhu Parekh's *A New Politics of Identity* (Palgrave 2008), though Parekh's take was slightly different.

12. J. Plamenatz, 'On Preserving the British Way of Life', in B. Parekh (ed), *Colour, Culture, Consciousness*, George Allen and Unwin 1974.

13. CMEB, *The Future of Multi-Ethnic Britain: The Parekh Report*, Profile Books 2000, pp23-6.

14. M. Swann, *Education for All*, HMSO 1986, pp7-8.

15. Brown speech, see note 3; Cameron speech see note 4.

16. S. Warsi, 'An Integration Nation: Breaking Down the Barriers', Operation Black Vote, 12.11.12, p3; Ed Miliband, 'Immigration Speech', IPPR, 22.6.12, p2.

17. See http://englishdefenceleague.org/about-us.

18. C. Joppke, 'Immigration and the Identity of Citizenship: the Paradox of Universalism', *Citizenship Studies*, 12: 6, 2008, p537.

19. QCA, *Citizenship: Programme of Study for Key Stage 3 and Attainment Target*, Qualifications and Curriculum Development Agency 2007, p33.

20. T. Modood, 'Post Immigration Difference and Integration', British Academy 2012, p40.

21. Joppke, 'Retreat ...', pp250-1; E. Vasta, 'Accommodating Diversity: Why Current Critiques of Multiculturalism Miss the Point', Working Paper No. 53, Centre on Migration, Policy and Society, University of Oxford 2007, p4.

22. N. Meer and T. Modood, 'The Multicultural State We're in: Muslims, Multiculture and the Civic Rebalancing of British Multiculturalism', *Political Studies*, 57, 2009.

23. Commission on Integration and Cohesion, 'Our Shared Future', CIC 2007, pp38-9.

24. T. Cantle, *Community Cohesion: A Report of the Independent Review Team*, Home Office 2001, p70.

25. C. Peach, 'Slippery Segregation: Discovering or Manufacturing Ghettos', *Journal of Ethnic and Migration Studies*, 35, 2009, p1389; G. Short, 'Faith-based schools: A threat to social cohesion?' *Journal of Philosophy of Education*, Vol 36 No 4, 2002; Finney & L. Simpson, 'Sleepwalking to Segregation', Policy Press 2009, pp127-8. Even for measures like faith schools, the arguments that that they promote separation and impede cohesion are notoriously weak.

26. V. Uberoi and T. Modood, 'Inclusive Britishness - A Multiculturalist Advance', *Political Studies*, Volume 61 (1) 2013.

27. B. Parekh, 'Postscript', in B. Parekh (ed), *Colour, Culture, Consciousness*, George Allen and Unwin 1974.

28. T. Modood, 'The Cricket Test: A Note to Mr Tebbit' [1990], in *Not Easy Being British*, Trentham Books 1992, p24.

29. David Miller, 'Reflections on British National Identity', *New Community*, 21, 1995, p164.

Has multiculturalism in Britain retreated?

30. *Parekh Report*, p229; E. Mclaughlin and S. Neal, 'Misrepresenting the multicultural nation: the policy process, news media management and the Parekh Report', *Policy Studies*, Vol. 25, No. 3 2004.

31. J. Straw, 'Speech at the Launch of the Parekh Report', *Runnymede Bulletin*, 324, 2000.

32. W. Hague, 'Identity and the British', speech, 19.1.99; and 'We Will Renew Britain's Civil Society', 2001.

33. Border Agency, *Citizenship Ceremonies*, 2010: www.ukba.homeoffice.gov.uk/britishcitizenship/applying/ceremony/; Home Office, *Life in the United Kingdom*, Stationery Office 2005, pp13-5.

34. QCA, *Citizenship*, p33.

35. Uberoi and Modood, *Inclusive Britishness*, p30.

36. J. Denham, 'Real and Imaginary Fears', *Prospect* 96, March 2004, p2.

37. M. Gove, 'What do Britons Have in Common?' Paper presented at Quilliam Foundation Conference, 23.4.09: www.youtube.com/watch?v=fwtXbw5n0vs; and 'Analysis: Britishness', BBC Radio 4, 14.6.10: www.bbc.co.uk/iplayer/episode/b00sny2h/b00snxy2/Analysis_Britishness/.

38. Conservative Party National and International Security Policy Group, *Uniting the Country: Interim Report*, Conservative Party 2007, p23.

39. D. Cameron speech, see note 4, pp4-5.

40. Uberoi & Modood, *Inclusive Britishness*.

41. Brown speech, see note 3, p2; Cameron, Munich speech, pp4-5.

42. L. Pal, *Interests of State: The Politics of Language, Multiculturalism and Feminism*, McGill Queens University Press, 1993; D. Goodha0rt, *Progressive Nationalism*, Demos 2005.

43. T. Modood, *Multiculturalism*, Polity 2007, p97.

44. W. Kymlicka, *Multicultural Citizenship*, Oxford University Press 1995, p188

45. B. Parekh, *Rethinking Multiculturalism*, Macmillan 2000, pp206, 219.

46. V. Uberoi, 'Social Unity in Britain', *Journal of Ethnic and Migration Studies*, 33, 2007; Finney & Simpson, 'Sleepwalking'.

47. W. Kymlicka, 'Comment on Meer and Modood', *Journal of Intercultural Studies*, 33, 2012, pp213-5.

48. T. Modood & N. Meer, 'How Does Inter-culturalism Contrast With Multiculturalism?', *Journal of Intercultural Studies*, 33, 2012, p235.

49. Y. Abu-Laban, 'The Politics of Race, Ethnicity and Immigration, The Contested Arena of Multiculturalism', in Bickerton & Gagnon (eds), *Canadian Politics*, Broadview Press 1999.

50. M. Lopez, 'The Origins of Multiculturalism in Australian Politics, 1945-75', Melbourne University Press 2000.

51. D. Miller, 'Immigrants, Nations and Citizenship', *Journal of Political Philosophy*, 16, 2008.

52. B. Parekh, 'Postscript', in B. Parekh (ed), *Colour, Culture, Consciousness*, George Allen and Unwin 1974, p230; D. Miller, *On Nationality*, Oxford University Press 1995, p143; J. Gray, *Gray's Anatomy*, Penguin 2010, p147.

53. D. Goodhart, 'The British are the New Irish', Demos 2012 [emphasis added].

54. V. Uberoi, 'Do Policies of Multiculturalism Change National Identities?', *Political Quarterly*, 79, 2008; and 'Multiculturalism and the Canadian Charter of Rights and Freedoms', *Political Studies*, 57, 2009.

55. Miller, *Immigrants, Nations and Citizenship*, p380.

When is peace?

Women's post-accord experiences in three countries

Cynthia Cockburn

What has happened to women's hopes for peace in Northern Ireland, Bosnia-Herzegovina and Israel-Palestine?

Peace is elusive. I don't mean that it eludes us in a practical sense - we think we have it, and then war returns. This is often so, of course. No. I mean in the sense that it's difficult to be sure what conditions we may confidently say add up to a time of peace.

In 1995-6 I went to interview peace-minded women in Bosnia-Herzegovina, Northern Ireland and Israel-Palestine. It was a time when peace agreements were in the air. In early 2012 I went back to revisit as many of the original women as I could find, and to ask them what had flowed from that hopeful moment.[1] I wanted to find out how their campaigns had fared in the intervening years - and what had become of peace.

****

The General Framework Agreement for Peace in Bosnia and Herzegovina, drafted at Dayton, Ohio, was signed in Paris on 14 December 1995, bringing an end to the series of ethnic secessions and aggressions that had destroyed Federal Yugoslavia. Eleven days later I sat down to Christmas dinner in Medica Women's Therapy Centre. Christmas dinner? In Muslim central Bosnia? Yes, because the

Soundings

staff of this extraordinary women's organisation, a medical, psychiatric and social resource for women raped and traumatised in the war - a clientele that was mainly Muslim - were an ethnically-mixed team. The majority were certainly Bosniak, as Muslims were now called, though that did not necessarily mean they had set much store by the fact before the identity was forced on them by nationalist demagogues mobilising Croatian and Serbian resurgences in the Yugoslav republics. They had been members of the League of Communists, most likely atheists. Very few would have adhered to a mosque. A minority of the Medica staff, however, were women of other 'names' - Bosnian Serb/Orthodox and Bosnian Croat/Catholic - or of mixed birth, or in mixed marriages. They had stayed put in Zenica, refusing to be intimidated into following the logic of the war by fleeing to territory secured by 'their' people in 'their' name. The Christmas dinner was not exactly an Orthodox or Catholic celebration, more an excuse, in a time of scarcity, to cook up something special and give presents all round. Having the privilege of living among them for a while, I tried to be usefully involved in Medica's information department - fundraising, using my camera and resources to make publicity materials, and passing on research knowhow. But my own purpose was to study and understand the thinking, processes and practices that enabled them to set aside the hugely divisive issues raised between them by the militarised nationalist projects of 'ethnic cleansing' in the region, and to work as a co-operative and feminist collective for the care of war survivors.

In Northern Ireland, that year of 1996, ceasefires were on the cards, and a peace process was gradually gearing up. It would culminate in the Peace Agreement signed on Good Friday 1998 that, although it could not right the wrongs of several centuries of colonial oppression, closed three decades of sporadic conflict. From the late 1970s there had been a move by women in many neighbourhoods of Belfast to open drop-in centres, a resource for local women. The city map is a patchwork of Catholic and Protestant housing areas, deeply divided by Republican and Loyalist affinities. Yet in a striking act of solidarity the women's centre of the deeply Protestant Shankill Road came to the support of the Falls Road women's centre when the City Council discriminated against the latter as supposed 'IRA supporters'. Thenceforth the two centres set up, with some other women's organisations and trade union input, a cross-community Women's Support Network. It became a feminist voice of working-class women in Belfast, finding common ground in the poverty, violence and political neglect besetting their neighbourhoods. Their co-

When is peace?

operation across conflict lines was condemned and punished by the armed groups controlling their streets. I stayed close to the Network for some months, to observe and learn from their deft and intelligent footwork in dealing with historical injustice, and the bitter contemporary divisions between them.

My project would later bring the Belfast women into contact, in a residential workshop and an exchange of visits, with the Bosnian women of Medica, and a third group with whom I was working in Israel-Palestine. There, the provisions agreed in the 1993 Oslo Accords, 'The Declaration of Principles on Interim Self-Government Arrangements', were gradually being implemented in the occupied West Bank, and giving cause for hope of an eventual settlement that would bring statehood, if not justice, to Palestinians. That same year, up in the north of the region, in the Galilee, the Jezreel Valley and the Wadi Ara, a group of Jewish and Palestinian women had started meeting. They demonstrated together in roadside 'Women in Black' vigils against the occupation. But, more than most 'peace groups', they called for full equality and democratic rights for the Palestinian minority within the state of Israel. They took the name Bat Shalom (Daughter of Peace), identifying themselves as a local branch of an organisation based in Jerusalem - though the latter did not share their emphasis on this internal issue. The Jewish members of Bat Shalom of the North lived on the agricultural *kibbutzim* and *moshavim* that spread across the fertile plains. The Palestinian women came from Nazareth, Umm el-Fahm, Ara and other densely inhabited Arab towns and villages confined to the unproductive hills. Neighbours though they were, these two peoples seldom came in contact. The cultural, economic and political disparities between them were great. And the historic injustice of Israel's theft of Palestinian land and expulsion of the majority of their community in 1948, followed by occupation in 1967 of the adjacent territories where many had taken refuge, was an enduring cause of antagonism in the Palestinians' relationship with the Jews among whom they lived. As with Medica and the Women's Support Network, my main research interest in Bat Shalom of the North was the processes and practices the women learned and employed in order to work together in a shared project of action, despite these sources of animosity.

I called my book about the three organisations *The Space Between Us*.[2] How did they cross that space - with words instead of bullets? That had been my question. So, revisiting the women sixteen years later, I hoped to find out what had become of that

Soundings

space, that distance between peoples thrown by political forces into ethno-national antagonism, in the wake of the peace accords of the 1990s. Is their dialogue any easier today? I did not expect violence to have ended altogether, but what trajectory had it taken, and with what effect on women attempting to prefigure peace?

Bosnia-Herzegovina

In Bosnia-Herzegovina I found Medica had lost its mixity. It was now almost entirely Muslim. The current director, Sabiha Haskić, had previously been Medica's Muslim religious counsellor. A second old friend I was equally delighted to find there was Ferida Djekić. Now the senior nurse, she is unique in today's Medica in being of mixed origin and in a mixed marriage. She said: 'I don't belong to any religious groups! I belong only to myself. Nobody sees me as Bosnian, Croat or Serb, because I don't allow it. I celebrate every holiday in the calendar, Christian, Muslim, whatever, to be a good example to the children. It's not a person's name, but how they behave that matters'.

It is not that the 'other others' have been driven away from Medica, far from it. It just happened, for lack of a policy to the contrary. In the post-conflict years, as Medica turned its attention from war victims to survivors of domestic violence, the staffing requirements changed. Some of those of Bosnian Serb and Bosnian Croat 'name' (I use this formula to reflect the women's distaste for ascribed identities) had been doctors or psychotherapists, and had gone

Little but apples in this local fruit market. In Zenica today people shop for basics, not luxuries.

When is peace?

back to their former jobs in the hospitals, or had moved on to apply their skills in other war zones. For some there had been families to raise, or they had fallen ill, or retirement age had arrived.

Rada Stakić, of Bosnian Serb 'name', who had worked in Medica as an interpreter during the war, was now teaching language skills in a university. She reminded me that she herself had never deemed Medica's mixity 'special', as I had done. For her it had simply been Yugoslav 'normality'. The civility they had sustained in the war, she said, continued to be unproblematic in the town of Zenica today, among 'normal' people. However, like the other seventeen women I re-interviewed this year in Bosnia, she was utterly dismayed and enraged by the relentlessly nationalistic tenor of postwar political culture in BiH. The Dayton Accord created a weak state, comprised of two strong entities, constitutionally ethnic, the Republika Srpska and the Federation of Bosnia-Herzegovina (subdivided into Bosniak/Muslim and Croat/Orthodox areas). Rather than diminishing nationalist enmity, this structure had fostered and rewarded it. Instead of any acknowledgment of guilt, any practice of transitional justice, irresponsible leaders could persist in mutual blame. The one or two political parties that do attempt to recruit from all 'names' and work for inclusive democracy have no hope of winning power. Throughout 2011 a nationalist deadlock made it impossible to form a government, so that the collapse of the state into bankruptcy and anarchy was only averted at the eleventh hour. The state survived into 2012, holding together by a thread. When I was there, in March, the armed men of all three sides were still enlisted

Second-hand books and tokens of love - a Zenica street scene, soon after Valentines' Day 2012.

Soundings

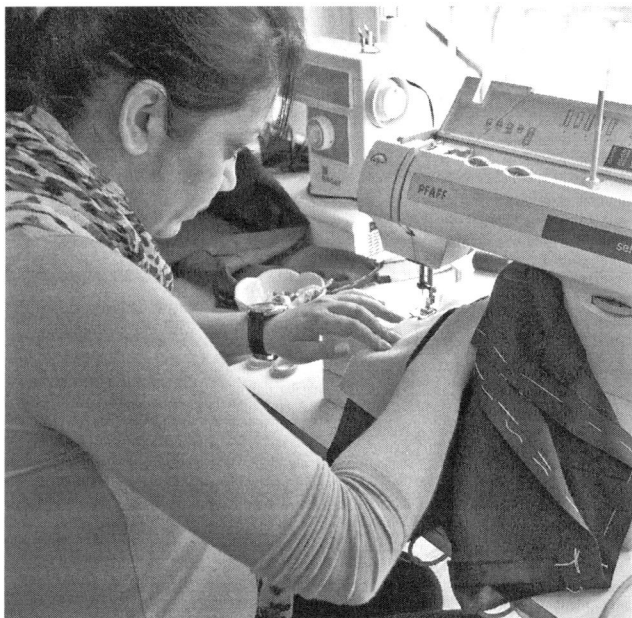

Zenica women's basketball team play visitors from Belgrade. Team loyalties express love of the game, bypassing politicians' nationalist rivalries.

Medica Women's Therapy Centre provide practical job training for women who come to them for refuge from domestic violence.

When is peace?

in a single postwar army, and I was told of a hopeful instance of cross-communal solidarity - former soldiers of assorted identity had been supporting each other in protest against non-payment of their pensions. Yet at the time of writing, late in 2012, there is talk of that unified army splitting apart, its fragments adhering to the nationalists that are pulling the country to pieces beneath its feet. Many fear a renewal of ethnic war prompted by Serb secession.

Meanwhile, for many women in postwar Bosnia, the gendered violence of the war that had torn towns and villages apart was now wrecking households. The postwar economic situation in BiH - characterised by poverty, joblessness and lack of prospects - provided a fertile base for the pathology of masculine violence. Many men, brutalised by the fighting, some by now experienced rapists, came back and turned the home itself into a battleground. Domestic violence and civilian rape became 'a widespread social problem ... and a serious breach of human rights'.[3] By the late 1990s, Medica had established a refuge for women surviving violence, and located themselves within an international movement of 'zero tolerance'. Jointly with other women's NGOs they successfully lobbied the government for laws to protect women. But when they accepted public funding and the partnership of the local council's Social Welfare Department, some women couldn't help feeling that feminist autonomy had been compromised.

Northern Ireland

In Northern Ireland I was shocked to find the walls of some Loyalist districts still disfigured by the old murals of men in black balaclavas wielding assault rifles - graphic intimidation that you might rather have expected, yet would not have found, in Bosnia. Indeed there were new murals, the paint still fresh, despite a well-meaning 'Reimaging Initiative' meant to wipe sectarian aggression off the city's walls. Many Belfast neighbourhoods, besides, are still divided by 'interfaces', high fences constructed to discourage raids into enemy territory. None of these so-called peace walls have been dismantled since the Peace Agreement, and indeed some have been built since that time.[4] True, the British Army is less in-your-face today, despite continuing sporadic assassinations of security personnel by the real IRA. In the main, the militarised masculinity that in Bosnia has been corralled within its unified army, in Northern Ireland has turned its weapons inwards. Loyalist gangs

Soundings

New high-rise developments lift the post-conflict city centre into European modernity.

fight each other for control of various illegal enterprises. Rebel Republicans bully young drug pushers in their own communities with a brutality they used to visit on collaborators or the enemy. Unemployed and demoralised men take it out on their wives and partners. As in Bosnia, rising domestic violence is a feature of 'peace' here.

In Belfast I spoke with thirteen of the women from my original study. Two of them were still co-ordinators of women's centres - the Windsor Women's Centre in the deeply Loyalist neighbourhood The Village, and Footprints, a centre in Catholic Poleglass. Sustaining the Women's Support Network's former practice of dialogue, they attempt a 'twinning' partnership. I asked them whether the risk involved in cross-community working was measurably less than it had been fifteen years ago. Gillian Gibson, co-ordinator of Footprints, said that, while it seemed acceptable now to exchange staff between the two women's centres, there was as yet little or no contact between their women users. The inhibition today comes primarily from the Protestant side; and it is not the choice of the women but the effect of the punitive stance of the men in these communities. Eleanor Jordan, co-ordinator of the Windsor Centre, confirmed that any contact with Footprints, or with other centres in Catholic areas such as the neighbouring Falls Road, much as they themselves welcome it, still has to be 'done in silence - we don't advertise it'. She noted a certain irony in this. In the Centre they urge women to have the courage to break the silence about male violence in their own lives:

> But the silence in this neighbourhood goes on unbroken. Nobody can leave their past behind them. You are still known for what you were.

When is peace?

Loyalist militancy still menaces the pedestrian who steps onto the 'wrong' pavement in Belfast.

Meanwhile, the Women's Support Network, in which Footprints and Windsor were once energetic protagonists, has lost its political feminist edge with the coming of 'peace'. It no longer challenges the politicians and the administration, turning the state's 'community development' into women's community empowerment. In a way reminiscent of Bosnia, the women's centres have obtained secure state funding. Management paperwork has taken over from campaigning as their budgets have grown to provide services for women and children. And they prudently desist from biting the hand that feeds them.

On the other hand, new developments like the Odyssey Arena, the Obel Tower and the massive Titanic centre make Belfast look pretty much like any other twenty-first century European city today. Of course, the Loyalist marching season still pits neighbourhoods against each other, but a shared public space is emerging. The women say that the centre of town today feels more like common ground than it once did. May McCann, a lover of folk music, tells me that the centre is developing slowly from a dark, gate-ringed, no-go area into a place where people of all religions and politics can come together in new venues, arts centres, bars and restaurants. The young, in particular, may be mixing more. A recent survey

Soundings

Footprints Women's Centre in Poleglass, West Belfast. The women and children grow vegetables in their own garden, cook them in the kitchens, serve and eat them in their community café.

showed that, despite the continuation of segregated schooling, today's sixteen-year-olds, the generation born after the 1994 ceasefires, are a tad more likely than their predecessors to cross the religious divide to make friends. Just one in five (22 per cent) today has no mates from the other main tradition, compared to one in three (33 per cent) in 2003.[5]

The 'power sharing' regime in Northern Ireland, the rigid tango Sinn Fein and the Democratic Unionist Party perform in each other's embrace, does not lend itself to spontaneous democracy with a vital left opposition. On the other hand it is a good sight more reassuring than Bosnia-Herzegovina's gridlocked nationalisms. And it certainly compares favourably with the situation in Israel, where the rift between the Zionist state and the political representatives of its subjugated Palestinians has grown steadily wider.

When is peace?

Israel-Palestine

In 1996, when I first spent time with the women of Bat Shalom, there was cautious optimism in the region. Although the Oslo Accords were disliked by the Jewish right and were felt by many Palestinians to be co-optative, they did constitute a promise of peace in the minds of many positive-minded people on both sides of the divide. It no longer seemed subversive to advocate a Palestinian state alongside the Israeli one. The transfer of some administrative powers to the Palestinian Authority was going ahead. But violent acts - including the assassination of prime minister Yitzak Rabin by a Jewish settler in November 1995 - had damaged confidence.

At that time I had well understood that the activist dialogue between Jewish women and Israeli Palestinian women in Bat Shalom, up there in the Galilee, was a highly unusual phenomenon, calling for political imagination and care. I should perhaps have been unsurprised to find, on my return in 2012, that there was no Bat Shalom at all. The hard worked 'space between' the women of the two communities had become thin air. The northern group had first split from the main organisation in Jerusalem in 2006, changing its name to Bat Zafon (Daughter of the North). Then, in 2008, it disbanded altogether. The Jerusalem office closed two years later. Seeking out the eight or nine former members I could still locate in the *kibbutzim*, in Nazareth and other Arab towns, I tried to uncover what had brought about the demise of their group.

Of course there was simply the attrition of time. We all grow

The Separation Wall defends new Jewish settlement in the occupied West Bank and impedes the movement of Palestinians.

Soundings

older, we get tired, we get sick and our activist energy falls away. But more than that, I could hear in their stories a gradual fading of hope. The scale of overt violence between the Israeli Defence Forces, Hezbollah in the north and Hamas in the south had escalated hugely over the decade. The 'second intifada' in 2000, the renewed invasion of Lebanon in 2006 and the brutal bombardment of Gaza in 2008-9 had been full-scale acts of war, their casualties in the thousands. Imposing the Occupation itself involved daily violence. The relentless militarised Jewish settlement in the West Bank had reduced and fragmented the area 'available' for a Palestinian state. Such a thing was no longer geographically feasible. There was no longer a peace process to support. It was not only Bat Shalom that had faded in this period. The whole Israeli peace movement was in eclipse.

The disillusionment and weariness that led women to withdraw from Bat Shalom had been felt most by the Jewish members. On the *kibbutzim*, attitudes had hardened. The intention of Bat Shalom of the North had always been to be an example in their home communities, to draw more local women into the dialogue. But now these activists felt themselves to be isolated on the *kibbutz*, hated even for seeking contact with 'Arabs'. The closure, for lack of funds, of Bat Zafon's small office in Afula had deprived the group of two full-time activists, and they had not managed to make the transition back to a fully volunteer organisation. However, the Palestinian women, particularly those who were active in the Nazareth branch of the sturdy and long-lived Tandi, the left-wing Movement of Democratic Women, were dismayed by the loss of their Jewish partners. They would have been prepared to continue. Instead, they persisted in their work of empowering Palestinian women and girls, and maintaining contact with those other Palestinians across the Green Line.

Interestingly, in its last few years of life, the northern group had radicalised, strengthened its practice and begun to envision a more daring programme of change in the region. Already, before the outbreak of the intifada in 2000, they had started to work together on annual events to mark Yom al-Ard - Land Day - important to the Palestinian community as marking the moment, in 1976, of the first uprising against the theft of Palestinian land by the Israeli state. It was a bold step for Jews to acknowledge this injustice and join Palestinians in organising around it. On Land Day this year, 2012, I was again in the Galilee. I went to the big rally held by Palestinians in the Arab town of Sakhnin, drawing thousands

When is peace?

of women and men, girls and boys, with massed flags of the political tendencies, the red hammer and sickle for Hadash, the Palestinian tri-colour for the more nationalist Balad. But there was no longer a mixed group of Jewish and Palestinian women with whom to mark the day.

In their last years, some of the women of Bat Zafon had come to be among the few in Israel's peace community who had dared to say openly that a two-state solution was no longer viable. The unthinkable must now be thought: relinquish the singular Jewish identity of Israel. Bat Zafon's women had always been convinced that true democracy within Israel was a necessary condition of a peace settlement in the region. Now they were ready to imagine a multicultural entity or entities across the whole Israel-Palestine region, from the Lebanon and Syrian borders in the north to the Egyptian border in the south, and from the Jordan river to the Mediterranean ocean, a nation of Jews, Palestinians and others in constitutional equality. But this vision gelled only at the moment the individuals of Bat Zafon dispersed and ceased active organising.

'Land Day', 30 March 2012, commemorated in Sakhnin, Galilee. Palestinians gather to protest the expropriation of Palestinian lands by the Israeli state.

Soundings

Former members of Bat Shalom of the North reconsider the days of the 'Oslo Accords' recalled in wall posters using photos and text from my previous visit.

Bat Shalom's failure was symptomatic of the feminist peace movement more generally. It had been an active member of the Coalition of Women for Peace, which, for its part, had often mobilised countrywide action against the Occupation and in support of peace moves. Today the Coalition is misnamed. It has become a single-focus organisation mainly involved in research. Women in Black, which once counted thirty vigils around Israel, has shrunk to three - in Jerusalem, Tel Aviv and Haifa. New Profile, a feminist organisation of women and men, continues its specific work in support of those who refuse military service. There are feminist groups such as Isha l'Isha in Haifa, whose concerns span women's rights, equality, the sex industry and the trafficking of women. But there is no successor project to Bat Shalom of the North, a sustained and tested partnership of Jews and internal Palestinians. Meanwhile, it is protest in the style of 'Occupy' - middle-class Jewish youth incensed by the growing gap between incomes and cost of living - that has taken the place on the city streets once filled by a movement to 'end the Occupation'.

When is peace?

The deferral of 'peace'

War brings untold suffering. But in some of its phases, as feminist students of war and peace processes have often pointed out, it affords some women scope for collective action that they lacked before.[6] This was the case in Northern Ireland, where the oppression of living in districts beset by street-level strife sparked a defiant working-class feminism. It happened in Bosnia-Herzegovina, when foreign funders and feminist activists, appalled by mass rapes, came to partner local women. And it happened in Israel-Palestine, a year into the *intifada*, when Jewish women were propelled into support of Palestinian women by their perception of the intolerable injustice of the Occupation. One form of active response to war that can be seen in the three women's organisations described above is an attempt to create and sustain a dialogue between women defined by the war-makers as enemies. Medica Women's Therapy Centre, the Belfast Women's Support Network and Bat Shalom of the North developed a practice that has since come to be known as 'transversal politics'. An issue of *Soundings* (No 12, Summer 1999) was devoted to this theme. We described it as a creative crossing and redrawing of boundaries that mark significant politicised differences, a process that can 'on the one hand look for commonalities without being arrogantly universalist, and on the other affirm difference without being transfixed by it'. It is relational *work* that calls for 'empathy without sameness, shifting without tearing up your roots'.[7]

Peace negotiations, however, characteristically overlook women and their transversalist insights. Notwithstanding the scale of sexual violence in the Bosnian war, women's representatives and women's issues were totally absent from that airfield in Dayton, Ohio, where international notables sat down with the war-criminal leaders in negotiations to end the fighting. 'Gender' was only introduced as a policy concern when, some time later, the Office of the High Representative, effective governor of postwar BiH, established a Gender Coordination Group of international agencies to work on equality issues. In the case of Israel-Palestine, not only were there no representatives of women at the table in the Oslo negotiations, the population of Palestinians living within the state of Israel were likewise absent from the talks, their interests in any future settlement ignored.

In Northern Ireland, however, the Good Friday Peace Agreement was the outcome of a more inclusive process, in which women's experience was allowed

Soundings

to make a difference. As the tense discussions proceeded between the political representatives of the British state and the warring parties, a movement in civil society, fostered by the European Union, mobilised to contribute ideas about a future Northern Ireland. The Women's Support Network, in alliance with others in a vibrant women's community sector, women trade unionists and a women's political party (The Women's Coalition) were able to insert themselves and their agenda into this process. The result was an accord that was not merely a truce between fighters but a commitment to a fair and inclusive society, with equality between Catholic and Protestant communities, equality between women and men, and on other grounds besides. As Beatrix Campbell wrote, in her impassioned book *Agreement!*, the Good Friday Agreement was 'a dynamic exemplar of reform democracy for the twenty-first century', embodying 'a transcendent duty to produce more than peace, to begin the millennial work of transforming the sectarian and sexist power relations that structure society'.[8] A decade and a half later, however, women say the devolved state structures of Northern Ireland are still failing to deliver on the promise. Here, as in Bosnia and Israel-Palestine, women are still asking 'When is peace, actually?'

All photographs taken by Cynthia Cockburn. For more information and more pictures: www.cynthiacockburn.org.

Notes

1. My thanks to the following trusts for their generous funding of this project: the Network for Social Change, the Feminist Review Trust, Lipman-Miliband (the Irene Bruegel Trust), the Lansbury House Trust Fund, the Scurrah-Wainwright Charity and the Maypole Fund.

2. Cynthia Cockburn, *The Space Between Us: Negotiating Gender and National Identities in Conflict*, Zed Books 1998.

3. Helsinki Citizens Assembly with other organisations, *Alternative Report on Implementation of CEDAW and Women's Human Rights in Bosnia and Herzegovina*, Banja Luka, Republika Srpska, BiH, 2010, p41.

4. Sean O'Hagan, 'Belfast, divided in the name of peace', Observer, 22.1.12.

When is peace?

5. Lindsay Fergus, 'More Northern Ireland teenagers crossing religious divide to make friends', *Belfast Telegraph*, 16.5.12.

6. For example, Medina Haeri and Nadine Puechguirbal, 'From Helplessness to Agency: Examining the Plurality of Women's Experiences in Armed Conflict', *International Review of the Red Cross*, Volume 92, No 877, March 2010.

7. Cynthia Cockburn and Lynette Hunter, 'Introduction: Transversal politics and translating practices', *Soundings* Issue 12, 1999.

8. Beatrix Campbell, *Agreement! The State, Conflict and Change in Northern Ireland*, Lawrence and Wishart 2008. Quotes from pp71 and 57.

New and forthcoming books from Lawrence and Wishart

On the Edge: The Contested Cultures of English Suburbia - Rupa Huq

'A fascinating exploration of the complexity and diversity of contemporary suburban life.' Jon Cruddas

Out now - ISBN 9781 907103 728 Price: £15.99

On the Wrong Side of the Track? East London and the Post Olympics - Phil Cohen

'a necessary, intelligent, and balanced response to a moment of local and national hallucination' Iain Sinclair

Publication date: April 2013 ISBN 9781 907103 629 Price: £17.99

London 2012: How was it for us? Ed. Mark Perryman

Contributors include: Yasmin Alibhai-Brown, Billy Bragg, Ben Carrington, Anne Coddington, Bob Gilbert, Kate Hughes, Suzanne Moore, Gavin Poynter, David Renton, Mark Steel, Zoe Williams.

'Mark Perryman's clear and concise outline of what the London 2012 games could have been is enthralling' LSE Review of Books

Publication date: June 2013 ISBN 9781907103797 Price: £14.99

Order books at: www.lwbooks.co.uk